Sunday School Smart Pages

REPRODUCIBLE
*Advice, Answers and
Articles About Teaching
Children Ages 2-12*

WES & SHERYL HAYSTEAD,

How to make clean copies from this book.

You may make copies of portions of this book with a clean conscience if:

✦ you (or someone in your organization) are the original purchaser.

✦ you are using the copies you make for a noncommercial purpose (such as teaching or promoting a ministry) within your church or organization.

✦ you follow the instructions provided in this book.

However, it is illegal for you to make copies if:

✦ you are using the material to promote, advertise or sell a product or service other than for ministry fund-raising.

✦ you are using the material in or on a product for sale.

✦ you or your organization are **not** the original purchaser of this book.

By following these guidelines you help us keep our products affordable. Thank you.

Gospel Light

Gospel Light

Contents

ARTICLES FOR EARLY CHILDHOOD: AGES 2-5

= Page number for related cartoon

Contents

Articles for Early Childhood and Children: Age 2-Grade 6

ARTICLES FOR EARLY CHILDHOOD AND CHILDREN: AGE 2-GRADE 6

Articles for Children: Grades 1-6

ARTICLES FOR CHILDREN: GRADES 1-6

✎ = Page number for related cartoon

Contents

ARTICLES FOR PARENTS AND TEACHERS

✎ = Page number for related cartoon

Contents

Dear Children's Leader, Think of This Book as Your—

1. Library of Resources
—Cataloged by subject, always at your fingertips, ready to assist you in providing your staff with vital, concise information about teaching children effectively.

2. Smart Pages
—Grab this manual when you need concise, down-to-earth information which can help a volunteer do a better job.

3. Tool Kit
—Stocked with useful, practical training helps which fit the needs of busy teachers—and leaders—of the children God has entrusted to your care.

4. Recipe File
—Filled with ideas you can use for a wide variety of occasions when your teachers need nurture for their vital ministry with children.

RECIPES

1.
Library of
Resources

2.
Smart
Pages

3.
Tool
Kit

4.
Recipe
File

Using This Book for Emergency Rescues

1. Place within reach.

2. Open when problems occur.

3. Skim Table of Contents.

4. Duplicate resource.

5. Distribute resource.

6. Discuss resource.

1. Place it within easy reach...with your most used resources.

2. Open it when a problem occurs for a member of your children's staff (i.e., a teacher's meeting is scheduled for tonight and you haven't had time to plan, an untrained teacher starts next Sunday, an untrained substitute will fill in next Sunday, the fifth-grade boys locked their teacher in the closet last Sunday, etc.).

3. Skim through the topical contents to find a listing for the problem at hand ("Closet, closet... no... delinquent... no... ah! Discipline!").

Notice that the book is divided primarily into age-level sections:

EARLY CHILDHOOD (AGES 2-5)

EARLY CHILDHOOD AND CHILDREN (AGE 2-GRADE 6)

CHILDREN (GRADES 1-6)

PARENT/TEACHER (RESOURCES FOR HOME AND CHURCH)

Check each section for the topic of interest—as well as the Mini-posters, Cartoons and Clip Art sections for aids in catching attention and reinforcing important points.

4. Duplicate as many copies of the resource(s) as needed.

The resources in this manual include:
✦ Concise and informative articles dealing with common problem areas
✦ Charts and worksheets to be used in avoiding or correcting problem situations
✦ Mini-posters to be displayed in classrooms, hallways and offices as reminders of key points about children's ministry
✦ Cartoons and clip art to add punch to your message

5. Distribute or display the resource(s).

6. With your staff, discuss the points raised in the resource.

Using This Book in a One-Year Plan for Communication and Training

1. From the Contents pages, select twelve major topics of value to your staff.

2. Schedule monthly (or at least bimonthly or quarterly) meetings with your staff, selecting one of the twelve topics for each meeting.

Choose one of these ideas for each meeting:

✦ Use the article(s) to prepare a presentation about the topic. Distribute copies for teachers to take home.

✦ Distribute copies of an article in advance of the meeting so teachers will be prepared to discuss ways to implement suggestions.

✦ Distribute copies of an article as teachers arrive. Teachers form small groups and discuss the article.

Here are some questions you can use to encourage discussion:

✦ What are some things the article mentions that you are already doing?

✦ How might your class be different next Sunday if you put into practice one idea from this article?

✦ What three ideas from this article are most helpful for your class?

✦ What difficulty might you face in implementing an idea from this article? Who can you talk to about ways to overcome this difficulty?

3. Select resources (articles, cartoons, mini-posters, clip art) from this manual to use in a monthly newsletter to communicate with your staff.

✦ Feature one of the twelve topics, coordinating with the staff meeting schedule.

✦ Identify major announcements and events to include in each issue.

✦ Identify several "human interest" features to catch attention (i.e., "Teacher of the Month," "Class in the Spotlight," "Ideas Worth Sharing," "Available Teaching Resources" [listing books, videos, filmstrips, supplies, etc. which correlate with the coming month's lessons], "Welcome to the Team" [introducing new staff members], etc.).

1.
Select
topics
of value.

2.
Use
topics at
meetings.

3.
Feature
resources in
newsletters.

A Sample One-Year Training/Communicating Plan

Monthly topics

Month	Topic	Page Numbers		
		Meeting	**Newsletter**	**Mini-Poster/Cartoon**
September:	**Characteristics**	23, 24, 103-107	37, 119, 159	209
October:	**Discipline**	25, 111	93	209
November:	**A Good Class Schedule**	57, 143	95	199
December:	**Telling Bible Stories**	67, 149	73, 75	197
January:	**Teaching & Learning**	45, 71, 123	89	211
February:	**Learning Activities**	17-21, 35, 39, 43 53, 63, 97 109, 113, 117, 127, 133, 145	15, 49, 61, 99	209
March:	**Guided Conversation**	41, 121	137	187
April:	**Salvation**	55, 141	179	211
May:	**Music & Rhythms**	47, 53, 127, 129		211
June:	**Summer Ideas**	69, 153		193
July:	**Building Relationships**	59, 139	171	195
August:	**Outreach/Attendance**	135, 155	181	201

Other Stuff to Do with This Book

1. Provide helpful information for parents as well as teachers.

✦ See the Parent/Teacher section (pages 155-183) for articles to help the church and home in working together to nurture children.

✦ Provide helpful insights about major seasonal events. Parents and teachers will appreciate your sharing ideas about Christmas, Easter and Halloween. (See pages 161, 163, 169 and 173.)

✦ Provide helpful insights about traumatic events. Death, divorce and remarriage pose major problems for children—and their teachers. These events can also result in times when children are most receptive to learning about God's love and care. (See pages 157, 165 and 167.)

✦ Use the cartoons and clip art to enhance the impact of your printed flier or newsletter.

2. Improve educational facilities.

Look under "Facilities" in the three age-level sections.

3. Help teachers:

✦ **make better use of curriculum resources.** (See page 13.)

✦ **minister to children with special needs.** Few churches have access to specialists in ministering to children who differ significantly from others their age because of disabilities. (See pages 65, 79-85 and 147.)

✦ **stimulate interest in Bible memory.** (See pages 73 and 101.)

✦ **nurture children in meaningful prayer**. (See pages 51 and 183.)

✦ **encourage missions awareness.** (See page 91.)

4. Provide selected articles to include in a packet for prospective and new teachers.

A few brief, thoughtfully compiled articles can make a new teacher's first sessions productive and enjoyable. The chart on the next page lists age-level articles you might use. Obviously, these aren't the only articles which are appropriate for a new teacher. However, it is better to give a new person a few items which he or she will read and remember than many items which will overwhelm the person and end up being ignored.

5. Let your own creativity (or desperation) stimulate you to think of other ways to use the resources in this manual. For example, tape record an article and distribute the cassette among your teachers and/or have it available to give to new teachers.

1.
Provide information for parents/teachers.

2.
Improve educational facilities.

3.
Help teachers improve skills.

4.
Inform new teachers.

Resources for New Teachers

Articles
for new
teachers

Getting the Most Out of an Activity Page

EARLY CHILDHOOD

What is the purpose of the Activity Page?

The Activity Page is an individual visual aid provided with your curriculum which usually illustrates one way children can apply a Bible truth to their own lives. The Activity Page often reviews key facts to help children remember the Bible story. These simple activities provide opportunities for teacher and children to engage in meaningful conversation.

What is the best way to introduce an Activity Page to children?

Before handing out pages, talk with the children about the pictures on the page so they understand its purpose. Demonstrate the steps children will take to complete their page (e.g., cutting, folding, gluing, etc.). Provide opportunities for children to talk about the scene or action on the page. Ask simple, specific questions to help children recall the action the page illustrates. Or begin the story, then ask, "What happened next?" Let a volunteer tell; then ask, "And then what happened?" Continue in this way until story is concluded. Involve as many children as possible.

In classes where learners are just beginning to use words to communicate, suggest a child answer your question by pointing to the appropriate figure on the Activity Page.

What is the best way to get all the pieces ready for the session?

Many churches have senior citizens or older children involved with weekday club programs who can do an excellent job of preparing Activity Page materials. At the beginning of each quarter these helpers separate the pages and punch out the stickers, placing them all in envelopes marked for each session.

How much help should a teacher give a child?

Try to assist only when a child cannot complete a task. Since each child's skill level is different, teachers should try to work with the same small group each week. Then the teacher can know which children may need extra help.

Is it necessary for every child to do an Activity Page each week?

If a child is not interested in doing the Activity Page, provide a quiet alternate task, such as drawing with crayons on blank paper or looking at books. Send the uncompleted Activity Page home and suggest that parents may invite the child to finish the page when interest is shown.

What should be done when there is a wide age and ability range in the group?

For the less advanced child, the teacher can begin a difficult task (i.e., folding), then the child can be allowed to complete it. Sometimes it is best to reduce the number of steps the child is asked to do. The more advanced child can be engaged in conversation about the scene or action on the page.

Some lessons suggest optional touch-and-feel materials to add to the Activity Page. Adding these optional materials provides more challenge for the advanced child.

Many teachers find it helpful to demonstrate how to complete the Activity Page before children are given their own pages on which to work.

How much creativity does a child experience in doing an Activity Page?

Activity Pages offer limited opportunities for creativity. The patterned nature of the page generally directs the children to specific rather than creative responses. The child's need for creativity can best be met with experiences during Bible Learning Activity time.

13

Kids Learn Best Through Activity

EARLY CHILDHOOD

How did you learn to ride a tricycle? Did your mom or dad sit you down and read the directions to you? No! Like every child, you probably climbed on the trike and learned by doing it yourself. Perhaps your first maneuvers were awkward. But with repeated attempts and by watching other young riders, you were soon pedaling down the sidewalk.

Let's apply this technique to learning Bible truths. It's not enough for a child to hear God's Word or even memorize it. He or she must *do* it! Direct, firsthand activity is the young child's most effective way to learn. The child must use all the God-given senses—touching, seeing, tasting, smelling and hearing—in order to learn efficiently. Adults who guide young children at church are compelled to help them learn Bible truths through active play experiences.

Bible Learning Activities suggested in your curriculum have been planned to help children learn Bible truths in the way they learn best—by being actively involved. To provide these here-and-now learning

opportunities, several ingredients are necessary. One is equipment and furniture appropriate for active youngsters. A second and more important ingredient is a teacher to guide the conversation and activity and to interpret scriptural truth in terms of the child's experience.

> *The child uses all the God-given senses to learn efficiently.*

For play to take on the qualities of a Bible Learning Activity, teachers *must* use words to describe ways children are putting God's Word into action. For example, the teacher assigned to the Home Living area can comment, "I like the way Ryan gave Jason a turn to use the broom. Ryan is doing what is right and good, just as our Bible tells us."

Words and actions need to be combined to help clarify and expand children's thinking. A child's hearing, thinking, speech and action are closely related.

> *Direct, firsthand activity is the young child's most effective way to learn.*

Often a teacher needs to begin the activity. As children become involved, the teacher stays alongside as an interested observer, using the lesson's Bible Words in natural conversation. Since children can move from one activity to another during Bible Learning Activity Time, the teacher may repeat the activity and conversation several times during the morning. (Although children are free to move from one area to another, encourage them to stay with one activity long enough to accomplish purposeful play. Should the child begin to flit from one area to another, a teacher needs to guide the child's actions in a more direct manner.)

Another ingredient necessary for a child's learning is adequate time. You'll notice that approximately half of the session is planned for Bible Learning Activities. (If your group consists of 2s and 3s, extend this time by five or ten minutes.) A child needs time to explore the use of materials and equipment and to establish relationships with children and with teachers.

As a child works with Bible Learning Activity materials, he or she will have repeated opportunities to share, take turns and show kindness. Each child will also be on the receiving end of these experiences. Bible Learning Activity Time provides a setting for children to develop Christian ways of behaving toward others. These lessons of love are not

EARLY CHILDHOOD

learned in a single experience. "Precept upon precept, line upon line, here a little, there a little" (Isaiah 28:10, *NKJV*) is the way a child learns. This kind of learning cannot be rushed!

Teachers also need time to observe children as they play. A child's casual comments, attitudes and behavior help show a teacher if that child has correctly understood the concepts already presented. For example, three-year-old Justin hears his teacher say, "Sharing is a way to do good things." However, when Justin grabs a truck from Joshua and says, "You share!" it is obvious he sees sharing as only something others do for him. His actions tell his teacher that Justin's idea of sharing needs to be expanded. After the teacher steps in to protect Joshua's truck, she can take Justin over to a table. "Let's play a sharing game," she can say as she shows Justin two flannel boards.

"I've got two flannel boards. I'll give you one. And I'll keep one. Then we'll take turns sharing the felt pieces. That's sharing." The teacher explains sharing with both words and actions as they enjoy the activity.

A teacher's honest encouragement and approval naturally follows a child's success. A smile or word of commendation helps a child feel satisfaction. These good feelings encourage the child to continue the learning experience. Be ready with specific expressions, such as, "I like the way Alex builds his block road." "Sara really knows about puzzles." "What a good helper Katie is! She put all the puzzles back in our rack!"

As you choose which learning activities to offer in your class, consider those for which you have space, teachers and equipment. If Bible Learning Activities are new to your group, begin with a large muscle activity, such as a Home Living area (perhaps the easiest to equip). Also, consider an activity—such as Art—which requires the child's use of smaller muscles. Then each quarter, plan for an additional activity area.

How Art Helps Children Learn Bible Truths

EARLY CHILDHOOD

Art experiences are among the most familiar—and most misunderstood—in a classroom for young children. Most young children are introduced to crayons very young, but few adults take the time to observe the child at work, to see the real value of what is being done. The key word in a young child's art experience is *process*—not *product*. The work the child puts into the experience is of more value than the finished product. The skills and attitudes and understandings a child gains far overshadow the price of paper that adults often make the object of much attention.

Art activities offer the young child an opportunity to give expression to thoughts and feelings. A happy, secure child may express happiness through the bright colors used in a painting. A shy or inhibited child may make just a few timid strokes with one finger on a finger painting. An angry child may release emotions by pounding, squeezing or twisting clay.

As a child works at art activities, he or she can learn basic concepts of sharing, taking turns, being kind and helping others. The child has opportunities to learn respect for the ideas and work of those about him or her. As a child and teacher use art materials together in a relaxed, creative way, opportunities for natural conversation with the child are likely to come. These "teachable moments" often are the best opportunities to help a child learn basic and vital scriptural truths.

Age-Level Characteristics

As in most areas of a young child's growth, artistic expression follows a pattern of development. Children under three begin to explore art materials to discover what happens. Strokes and movements are often uncontrolled. Children's art at this stage should not be labeled "just scribbling." Rather, it is an important step toward developing control and learning appropriate use of materials.

The art work of children over three is usually under greater control. The child knows what the materials will do and has a definite—though often changing—purpose in mind. Gradually the child becomes capable of actually expressing and representing certain ideas. However, experimentation remains an important value for the child. The child gets real pleasure from making interesting lines, shapes, patterns and designs, and periodically announces the production of some object, animal or person. Eventually the child begins to make this announcement *in advance* of doing the work. Inevitably the day arrives when adults can recognize the intended result, but even then it is wisest (and safest) to avoid saying what you think a child has just made.

The Teacher's Role

The teacher's role is clearly to encourage the child's efforts in each stage of development. It is extremely important for the teacher to focus on the *process* of the art experience, and *not* on the finished product! Do not insist on perfection or correctness from an adult perspective. Avoid "improving" or "finishing" a child's work.

Encourage children to do things for themselves. When a child says, "Draw a tree for me," suggest, "First, let's see how much you can do by yourself." Should the child become frustrated, suggest, "I think it might be a good idea for you to start by coloring some green grass."

Always write the child's first

How Art Helps Children Learn Bible Truths

(Continued.)

name on artwork so it can be easily identified. Allow the child to write his or her name whenever possible, even if all the child can do is write the first letter.

The emphasis in Art Bible Learning Activities should be to give each child enjoyable and lesson-related art experiences. Art experiences are helpful means for Bible learning, not only by allowing children to illustrate Bible truth, but also through the child's activity while completing a project.

As teacher and child work together, opportunities for natural conversation provide "teachable moments" for children to learn important scriptural truths. For example, as children use colored chalk to draw designs on construction paper, sharing materials will come naturally. You can reinforce Jennifer's sharing by describing her actions. "Jennifer,

you let Ben use the blue chalk. That was a kind thing to do. Sharing is one way to be a kind friend. Our Bible says, *A friend loves at all times.*" Add a smile to your words. Look for opportunities to help children demonstrate kindness. "Lupe, Wesley doesn't have enough room for his paper. What could you do to help him?"

Every child needs a teacher who is friendly and understanding about his or her art work. Art activities help the child learn basic Christian concepts of sharing, taking turns, being kind and helping others. Art activities create opportunities to learn respect for the ideas and work of other children as well.

Building Blocks of Learning

EARLY CHILDHOOD

Blocks are important learning tools for all young children. Block building helps a child develop physically, mentally, socially and spiritually. Building with blocks allows a child to work alone, parallel to another child, or in cooperation with others in a small group. Most young children prefer building alone or next to another child.

Lifting and carrying blocks helps satisfy a child's need for large muscle activity. Building with blocks also helps a child to develop his or her own ideas and learn to make decisions. A child also learns how to care for materials.

When young builders work in small groups, they will have opportunities for cooperation and sharing. Children learn to respect the rights and ideas of others. All have opportunities to cooperate in problem solving and decision making. Block building provides firsthand experiences in practicing concepts such as sharing, helping, taking turns and exercising self-control.

In addition, block building allows teachers to observe children being themselves, actively having fun. Invariably opportunities arise for the teacher to help children learn to resolve conflicts in ways that promote respect for one another.

The Teacher's Role

How can the teacher assigned to the block area use this activity to teach Bible truths? A teacher's conversation with young builders can help children *know* and *do* what God's Word says.

For example, in a lesson focusing on obedience to God's Word, your curriculum might suggest building a block "wading pool" large enough for several children to get inside. The conversation ideas relate this activity to obeying. "Adam, have you ever played in a wading pool? Does your family have rules about playing in a wading pool?" The teacher listens carefully to determine family rules for water play. "When your mom says, 'Do not play in the pool without me there,' what do you remember to do? You obey! Why is it very important for you not to play alone in the water?" Again, the teacher listens attentively to children's comments. "Our Bible gives special rules to boys and girls. One of those rules is, *Children obey your parents.* I'm glad you obey your parents."

As block play continues, the teacher asks simple questions to help children recall other family rules. "If a ball rolls into the street, what should you do? Where do you ride your bike? Your parents love you very much. They want you to obey so you can play safely. *Children obey your parents* is what our Bible says." Again and again, the teacher uses the Bible verse in natural conversation.

Occasionally, a block-building project will help children become familiar with Bible-time life. For instance, in a lesson when a house will be mentioned in the Bible story, the teacher guides children in building a house with blocks, cardboard pieces and folded paper "stairs." Children "walk" small figures up the stairs to the flat roof. Later in the lesson when the children hear about a Bible-time house, the concept will be familiar. This block-building activity will give children increased understanding of the Bible story.

(Continued.)

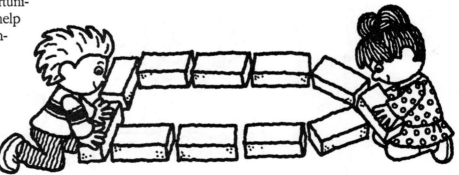

Building Blocks of Learning

(Continued.)

Age-Level Characteristics

Expect a two-year-old to hold a block or carry it around. The child may hold one in each hand and bang them together or pile one block on top of another and knock it down. A two-year-old usually enjoys playing alone or watching others build.

A three-year-old often uses several blocks at a time. He or she may stack them merely for the pleasure of stacking. Or the child may name the construction, changing its identity from moment to moment. Three-year-olds are most often seen playing alone.

The four- or five-year-old is beginning to plan what to build and how to build it. The child uses imagination in playing out actions with the construction. Fours and fives enjoy using accessory toys such as boats, trucks and small figures in their play. A building may have doors, windows and a roof. Block-building activities will range from watching, playing alone, etc., to cooperative planning and play.

Kinds of Blocks

Blocks for children under three should be lightweight and easy to manipulate. Suitable blocks can be made from empty milk cartons and cardboard boxes. Provide enough blocks so several children can build at the same time.

Fours and fives need a larger number and variety of blocks. A set of wooden unit blocks is a versatile learning tool that stimulates creative building.

Accessory Toys

Children under three tend to use each toy—a block or a truck—independent of other toys. However, older children will enjoy using accessory toys in the same area with the blocks. The value of block building is enhanced by a variety of accessory toys which encourage dramatic play. Sturdy transportation toys should be a part of every block area. (Wooden cars and trucks are preferable to most metal ones for safety and durability.)

Other accessory toys include stand-up figures of people, animals and trees. Fours and fives enjoy using signs ("Airport," "Gas Station," "Stop" and "Go") in dramatic play.

Storing Blocks

Blocks and accessory toys should be neatly arranged on low, open shelves, making it easy for children to see and help themselves. Avoid using a bin to store the items. If your classroom has no open shelves, use cardboard boxes. Place boxes on their sides with open ends out. Establish the practice of stacking blocks by shape and size. Attach a piece of adhesive paper to the front of every shelf, cut the size and shape of the blocks which belong there. Teachers need to consistently guide children in this cleanup procedure.

Building Guidelines

Guide children to build several feet away from the block shelves so others may get to the blocks without knocking down someone's construction. A strip of masking tape on the floor about two feet from the shelves makes a good silent reminder.

The floor of the block area should be carpeted with a smooth rug to provide a warm, level surface for building, while at the same time reducing noise.

Consider this rule to avoid injuries: "No one stacks blocks higher than his or her chin."

Read Me a Story!

EARLY CHILDHOOD

"Read it again!" is the best compliment a young listener can give to the teacher at the Book activity. It means that the child thoroughly enjoyed looking at the pictures, hearing a brief story or naming the items in the illustration with the help of an interested adult.

Books are important learning tools for all children. Using books with children provides opportunities to relate Scripture truth to areas of interest and experience.

Books delight children, helping them create ideas and stimulating their curiosity. Books encourage awareness of words. Happy experiences with colorful, interesting books help create a desire to read.

Books and teaching pictures for young children are very effective in stimulating and reinforcing Bible learning when they relate to a specific lesson focus and/or Bible verse.

Age-level Characteristics

Children under three are still primarily interested in pictures. The child will often point to one object in a picture and name it. Although younger children are usually eager to go on to the next page, they enjoy responding to simple questions about the illustrations. Books for twos and threes should have few words on each page. Stories should be about familiar subjects (such as animals, babies and families) and about family activities (such as playing, helping, eating and sleeping).

Fours and fives are also primarily interested in the pictures in a book, but enjoy hearing a brief story as well. Select storybooks with no more than a few sentences on a page. Many children are aware of the words on a page. "What does that word say?" a child may ask. Fives are learning to recognize some words and may happily announce, "I know that word! It's 'stop'."

Fours and fives enjoy stories and pictures about family, home and friends, but they are also interested in stories about nature, machines and people from other lands. Simple stories about Jesus should be included for all ages.

A Bible is the most important book in your room. You may provide a large Bible with Bible story pictures taped next to the Scripture passage for the day.

Arrange books in a quiet area of the room. A child may browse through a book alone or join two or three others to listen to a story. A teacher needs to remain nearby to read the text or talk about the pictures; otherwise, a child may become bored in a few seconds.

The Teacher's Role

Sit on the floor or at a low table. Interest children in the book or teaching pictures by looking at them yourself. Make comments aloud, such as, "I wonder why this little boy is looking sad." Soon children will come to see what you are doing.

As you turn the pages of a book, ask simple questions to help children "see" picture details. For example, ask, "What does this cow have around her neck? Find another cow with a bell around her neck." Also, ask open-ended questions such as, "Where do you think this boy and his dad are going?" Asking "What do you think?" questions encourages children to respond. Because there is no right or wrong answer, even very shy children will soon feel safe in sharing their ideas.

Teachers can also help build a child's vocabulary by repeating the child's reply in a complete sentence and by occasionally adding a word. "Anna, what is this? You are right! It's a bird. It's a red bird. God made the birds."

21

Characteristics of 2s and 3s

EARLY CHILDHOOD

Physical

From two to three years the child is in constant movement. The child tumbles often. Large muscles are developing, but small hand/finger muscles are not developed. Twos walk, climb,

scribble on paper, build a tower with blocks, turn pages of a book, feed themselves snacks. Threes may build structures with blocks, draw pictures which they will name as objects/people, begin to count, and may begin to use scissors on heavy, straight lines.

Teaching Tips: Plan for freedom of movement. Use simple finger fun and activity songs for stretching, stepping, jumping, clapping. Use simple puzzles, large blocks, jumbo crayons and large sheets of paper. Provide some quiet-time activities.

Mental/Emotional

Twos have short attention spans. They may say many single words and some sentences. The child is beginning to recognize his or her name in print. Two- and three-year-olds are explorers; they learn through their senses. They can learn rhymes, songs and finger fun.

Teaching Tips: Provide materials with interesting textures, smells, tastes, etc., for the child to explore. Use literal, simple stories with no symbolism. Be brief and use pictures or flannelgraph figures often. When telling them what to do, give one brief direction at a time. Wait patiently until they have responded before you continue with the next direction.

Social

Twos have little regard for the rights of others. Threes can interact in play with others. However, it's still a "ME, MY, MINE" world. Sharing and taking turns is hard to do. When a conflict arises, children respond better to distraction rather than reasoning.

Teaching Tips: Teachers need to be kind and patient. Offer opportunities for play with other children. Know each child as an individual and use his or her name often. Help each child to succeed by providing activities appropriate for the child's abilities.

Spiritual

The two- and three-year-old can learn that God made all things and that God cares for him or her; that Jesus is God's special Son and that He did kind, loving things when He lived on earth; that the Bible is a special book about God and Jesus and that Bible stories are true.

Teaching Tips: The child's learning about God is dependent on not only what people say, but also what people show about God. Your loving actions help the child understand God's love. Help the child experience God's presence in our world through a variety of seeing, touching, smelling, tasting and hearing activities. Talk and sing about God.

Characteristics of 4s and 5s

EARLY CHILDHOOD

Physical

At this age children are in a period of rapid physical growth. Coordination is greatly improved. These children are still constantly on the move! Girls often mature more rapidly than boys. Fours and fives may be able to cut with scissors on a curved line and draw recognizable pictures of people and objects. **Teaching Tips:** Freehand, creative art activities are best. Don't expect perfection. Children this age still need to be recognized for their work on the process of art, not the product. Large pieces of paper, jumbo crayons and heavy lines for cutting are needed. More sophisticated toys are appropriate: puzzles with 10-20 pieces, varieties of construction toys (various shapes and sizes), realistic home living accessories (dress-up clothes for boys and girls, kitchen utensils, food packages), etc.

Mental/Emotional

Fours and fives are curious and questioning. They may concentrate for longer periods, but their attention span is still short. Children will interpret your words literally. Fours and fives may recall short Bible verses, talk accurately about recent events and pronounce most common words correctly. **Teaching Tips:** Use large teaching pictures to reinforce basic concepts. Set realistic limits

and emphasize the behavior you desire. ("Ryan, running is a good thing to do outside where there is lots of room. Inside we have to walk so no one will get hurt." "Chantel, you may only draw on your own paper. Are there any more places on your page that you want to make purple?") Supply a variety of materials for children to touch, see, smell and taste. Help children discover things for themselves by having the freedom to experiment (play) with a variety of safe materials.

Social

The four- or five-year-old child can participate with other children in group activities. The child actively seeks adult approval, responds to friendliness and wants to be loved, especially by his or her teacher. Some children may use negative ways of gaining attention from others. **Teaching Tips:** Provide opportunities for group singing, prayer and conversation. Give each child a chance to "lead" by serving a snack, holding a picture, etc. Give each child individual attention before negative behavior occurs. Make eye contact often, listen carefully to the child, smile and show that the child is special to you.

Spiritual

The four- and five-year-old child can learn basic information about God—He made the world; He cares for all people; He forgives him or her when the child is sorry for doing wrong. A child this age can also learn that Jesus died to take the punishment for the wrong things we have done and that He rose from the dead and is alive. Fours and fives can be taught that the Bible tells us ways to obey God and that he or she can talk to God in prayer. **Teaching Tips:** Because the child still thinks literally and physically, avoid the use of symbolic words, such as "born again," "open your heart," or "fishers of men." When about to use a symbolic expression, think of the simplest, literal explanation you could give of what the expression means. Then use that simple explanation *instead* of the symbolic one which may confuse the child. Some children may respond to individual conversations by praying to become a member of God's family. Provide opportunities for children to hold the Bible.

Why Do They Act Like That?

"What a morning this has been!" comments a bewildered teacher.

"Why can't little children sit still?" sighs another. "What these kids need is discipline!"

Why is a child's behavior sometimes puzzling and frustrating? Why *do* children "act like that?"

No two children are alike. We cannot begin to number the different experiences each child has had in the first six years of life. Nor can we fathom the varying expectations that families have placed upon these children. And yet—knowing these things—we continue to be surprised when children do not act the way we have anticipated they will act.

By the same token, no two teachers are alike. And yet most of us, when surrounded by a roomful of children, are painfully alike. We want children to *behave*—which usually means we want them to act the way we anticipate they will act!

Where can the weary teacher find help? Is discipline the answer? And just what *is* discipline?

> *Discipline is the guidance a teacher gives so children learn to control their impulsive behavior.*

Freedom Within Limits

Good discipline is what you do *with* and *for* a child, not what you do *to* him or her. Discipline, then, is the guidance a teacher gives so a child knows what he or she *may* do as well as what he or she *may not* do.

For a child to grow into a thoughtful and loving adult, he or she needs to begin developing self-control—direction from within. To accomplish this life-long task, the child needs loving and understanding adults to guide behavior until he or she is mature enough to handle the task alone.

Learning to get along with others and to use materials and equipment creatively help a child enjoy the beginning of his or her church school experience. A child has (hopefully) many years of church attendance ahead. How important, then, that these first experiences be pleasant ones! To establish a positive learning atmosphere, consider these guidelines:

Love and care for each child. This love is not the gushy kind, but a love that gives a child what he or she needs to grow and develop. Children long to feel that someone cares about them, that

they are people of worth and value. Demonstrate your love and care in ways a child can understand. Sit down at the child's eye level and listen attentively to what a child has to tell. Kindly but firmly redirect a child's out-of-bounds activity. When you redirect a child's disruptive or unacceptable activity, do not scold or shame the child. Scolding or shaming makes the child feel excluded from your love. Focus on the child's *behavior*, not on the person. Let the child know you love him or her, but that you cannot allow the misbehavior. In all your actions and words, reflect the unconditional love you yourself have experienced from God.

Plan an interesting schedule of activities. If you expect children to sit quietly and "wait for class to begin," then you are asking them to act like miniature adults. Normal young children often misbehave simply because they are bored. Young children need action. As they grow and learn, they *must* move around. They learn best by touching and testing everything around them. For this reason, it's best to offer a variety of Bible Learning Activities from which children can choose.

Help children feel a sense of security and order. Tell them by your actions and your words that they are safe in your care and that you will allow no harm to come to them. Children also find security in knowing you are nearby to

assist when they need help. When they are assured you will be there to help, they will be more willing to try a new activity or experience.

Children like to be fairly sure of what will happen next. Follow the same schedule of activities each week. Of course, there will be times when you will need to be flexible by shortening or lengthening parts of the schedule, depending on the interest and attention spans of the children.

A child feels secure with limits. He or she needs to know what you expect. Establish a few basic rules, such as, "Dough stays on the table." Phrase the rules in a positive way whenever you can. Help children remember and observe the rules during their work and play. Give each child consistent and positive guidance. Find a middle ground between rigid authority and total permissiveness. Children need limits; but they also need freedom to move around and make choices within those limits.

Children respond in a positive way to a neatly arranged room with fresh and interesting things to do. When the same old stuff is in the same old places, with pieces missing or parts broken, this scene is almost certain to invite misbehavior.

When a child receives an adult's thoughtful and consistent guidance, he or she is on the way to understanding what it means to be responsible for one's own behavior. From this responsibility grows self-control—discipline from within.

Control Unacceptable Behavior

Sometimes a teacher's most thoughtful preparation and guidance does not keep a child from misbehaving. With most preschoolers, you have only about 10 seconds to do the correcting. Avoid long explanations. There are no surefire guarantees for these special situations. However, here are brief suggestions to guide you:

When a child hits (kicks, scratches):
"That hurts. I cannot let you hit Shannon. And I cannot let Shannon hit you. You may not hurt other people here. *Tell* Shannon what you want." Separate the two children. Redirect the offender's activity to another area of the room. Stay with the child until he or she is constructively involved.

When a child bites:
"Biting hurts. We use our teeth only to chew food." Never encourage a child to bite back to "show how it feels."

When a child spits:
"Your spit belongs in your mouth. If you need to spit, you may spit in the toilet."

When a child uses offensive names:
"Do not call Alex stupid. He is not stupid. He is drawing the way he thinks is best. Alex is doing a good job of drawing. And you are doing a good job of drawing."

When a child has a tantrum:
This is no time for words. The child is too upset to listen. Hold the child firmly until he or she calms down. When you hold the child, you are offering protection as well as control. If other children are frightened by the tantrum, take the child to another room with an adult to supervise. Explain to children, "Katie is having trouble now. She will be all right in a little while."

(Continued.)

> *Set limits to help children feel a sense of security and order.*

Why Do They Act Like That?

(Continued.)

EARLY CHILDHOOD

Redirect Distracting Behavior

Activity does not prevent a child from listening or learning. When a child's "active-ness" is not interfering with another child's attention, let that child do what his or her energy is requiring at that time. However, there are some general guidelines that can help limit distractions during large group times.

If a child's activity is interfering with another child, signal a teacher or helper to sit beside or behind the active child. The teacher can gently guide arms and legs back into the active child's own space, or provide a productive alternate activity the child can do. ("Timmy, if you want to stay here next to John, you must keep your hands in your own lap. Or, would you rather come and look at a book?")

Simply state what the child is to do with his or her hands. It is often appropriate to tell the child what will happen if he or she continues to disturb (e.g, be moved to another place).

If the disturbing actions continue, do *exactly* what you said you would do. Your effectiveness depends on your ability to follow through on your promise.

If more than one child is showing signs of restlessness, realize that it's time to do something else (e.g., sing an activity song, stand and stretch, etc.).

When a child consistently misbehaves during activities, remove the child from the scene of the difficulty. "Joshua, books are for looking at, not for tearing. We do not tear books. I have to put away the books." "Amy, you need to come to the puzzle table. I see the puzzle with horses on it that you like." Keep conversation cheerful.

Help the child handle negative feelings by accepting them. "Lupe, I know you feel angry at Jennifer for knocking down your blocks. But you may not hit Jennifer and Jennifer may not hit you."

Watch to determine what makes the child want to continue negative behavior. Sometimes misbehavior is simply a bid for attention. Quite often a child would rather be punished (which is one way to get adult attention) than receive no attention.

Avoid repeated threats. There is a difference between a threat ("Wesley, if you do that again, I will...") and explaining consequences ("I cannot let you do that because it might hurt someone."). A threat is a form of a dare that increases tension, while an explanation of consequences (in terms a child can understand) defines limits.

> *Substitute a new activity along with your firm statement about unacceptable behavior.*

Tight Space Solutions for the Classroom

EARLY CHILDHOOD

Dear Editor,
Your curriculum has wonderful activities, but we're in a small building with limited space in our classrooms. How can we adapt these activities to our limited space?
Signed,
Tight Space

If you've asked the same question, here are some **general suggestions.**

1. First, remove any unnecessary furniture (e.g., piano, large tables, extra chairs, etc.). Sometimes classrooms unwittingly become storage areas for unwanted items.

2. Build wall-mounted shelves 50 inches (125 cm.) above the floor to free up any floor space currently being used for storage.

3. Put items not in use out of children's reach. Reserve low shelves for materials children will use in the current session.

4. If necessary, provide space for teacher storage outside the classroom (a hallway cupboard, closet, supply room, etc.) to free up space for children's activities.

Here are some **specific suggestions** for adapting Bible Learning Activities to your limited facilities.

Art

Painting: Spread newspapers over a section of the floor (away from the flow of traffic in your room). Paintings may be done on paper placed on newspapers. If weather permits, children may paint outside. Allow pictures to dry outside. Or string clothesline in the hall or high in the classroom. Attach pictures to line with clothespins. For cleanup, provide paper towels and two plastic tubs half full of water. Children wash paintbrushes in one tub and their hands in the other. You may wish to substitute crayons, felt pens, or chalk for paint in the Art activities.

Murals: Attach paper to the wall with masking tape or thumbtacks. Place pictures, glue and scissors on small trays. Children complete activity without taking up valuable table space. Or children may work on the floor to complete a mural or collage.

Blocks

If you have limited space for storing blocks or for building with blocks, purchase small wooden or plastic "alphabet blocks" that easily fit in small hands. Less storage space will be needed and children will still be able to build any of the structures suggested in the block activities.

Books

Display only those books which highlight the lesson focus. These may be displayed along a section of the wall or in a small bookrack. Teacher and children may sit on the floor or on carpet squares (available from carpet stores) to read.

God's Wonders

If table space is not available for a God's Wonders activity, use a shallow box or tray in which to place items. Children relax on the floor or sit on carpet squares as they look at items. For planting activities, use trays placed in a less traveled area of the room.

Home Living

Doll and cooking play may be done on table tops instead of in a special Home Living area. For cooking play provide pans, spoons and other utensils. Use masking tape to section off a portion of the table for a stove. Use a plastic dish pan as a sink. Push two chairs together for a baby bed. Place dress-up clothes in a box or small suitcase. Store box until clothes are needed. Drape blankets over tables to make tents. Stores can be set up on table or floor by stacking empty boxes for shelves.

(Continued.)

EARLY CHILDHOOD

EQUIPMENT IDEAS

Tight Space Solutions for the Classroom

(Continued.)

Rhythms

If rhythm instruments aren't available, they can be easily made. Tie small bells together with string or ribbon. Children shake bell strings. Empty coffee cans with plastic lids make nice drums. Children tap lids with fingers. Use dowels or unsharpened pencils for rhythm sticks. Small wooden blocks covered with sandpaper make rhythm blocks when two are rubbed together. Provide a metal pan lid as a "cymbal" that children tap with a dowel.

Skill Toys

If table activities take up too much space, remove the table. Activities can be done easily by children sitting on the floor.

Remember—children have great imaginations. Even when the materials are not elaborate, children will still have meaningful learning experiences.

> *Remember—children have great imaginations. Even when the materials are not elaborate, children will still have meaningful learning experiences.*

User-Friendly Rooms for Young Children

EARLY CHILDHOOD

Young children need open space and a wide variety of materials. Make sure the room furniture is the proper size: chairs—10-12 inches (25-30 cm); tables—20-22 inches (50-55 cm); and table tops—30x48-inches (75x120-cm) to 36x60-inches (90x150-cm).

The most important feature of a room for young children is the clearly defined learning activity areas. These are places in the room where a teacher and children can actively explore and experiment.

BLOCKS, GAMES and SKILL TOYS help a child learn to reason and solve problems as well as develop coordination. These activities bring pleasure and, with guided conversation from a sensitive teacher, will stimulate curiosity about church, family, the world, God and Jesus. GOD'S WONDERS activities help children understand the world God made. As the teacher guides the conversation, the children also learn of the care provided by their parents, teachers and God. Dramatic play in the HOME LIVING area and looking at pictures at a

BOOK corner help children relate their everyday lives to the Bible truths they learn at church. ART and RHYTHM experiences help children express their feelings and ideas.

A well-designed room for young children is equipped to provide all of these experiences. In most cases, all of these activities would not be available in any one session, but each could be offered at different times.

In addition to these activity areas, the room should also allow all teachers and children in the department to meet together for a time of music, sharing and group activities. The Bible story can also be told in this large group time. From the large group, teachers and children then move into small groups to complete the Activity Pages. These groups can either sit around tables or on the floor. Dividers between groups are usually not necessary.

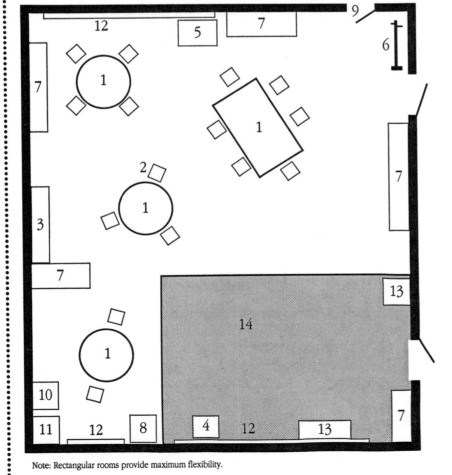

1. Table
2. Chair
3. Book Rack
4. Cassette Player
5. Painting Easel
6. Coatrack
7. Open Shelf Unit
8. Doll Bed
9. Rest Room
10. Child Stove Unit
11. Child Sink Unit
12. Bulletin Board
13. Small Table
14. Rug

Note: Rectangular rooms provide maximum flexibility.

Catch a Child's Imagination

EARLY CHILDHOOD

This is our world,
our big, big world,
And these are the
mountains high.
This is a tree,
a tall, tall tree,
And this is a bird that flies.
This is the sun,
the bright, bright sun,
That shines and
keeps us warm.
This is our world,
our big, big world,
And God has made it all.

by Anne Christenberry

The joy of repetition, the easy rhythm, the physical activity, the fun of pretending—all are natural expressions of a young child. What a great way to teach Bible truths!

Finger fun is an integral part of curriculum for young children because:

A child enjoys imaginative rhythmic actions. Through finger fun, he or she can pretend to be a sheep, a flower or a tree blowing in the wind. Finger fun provides a way for pretending to climb a ladder, swing high in the air or float to the ground like a snowflake.

A child needs an active form of expressing what he or she is learning or has learned. Through finger fun, children can dramatize Bible story events and become part of the action.

A child needs time for large muscle activity to alternate with periods of inactivity (listening). Finger fun provides meaningful activity for muscles weary from sitting still.

A child needs to relate the Bible teaching focus to his or her own experiences. Finger fun helps demonstrate ways to show love and kindness.

Guidelines for Using Finger Fun

✦ Before you use the finger fun suggested for a lesson, know it well yourself. Practice it at home.

✦ Speak the words rhythmically, yet distinctly. Begin slowly and increase tempo as children become familiar with the finger fun.

✦ Use actions words and sketches suggest. You may want to make up additional actions or use the actions suggested by a child.

✦ Repeat the finger fun several times during the session. Plan to include it in future lessons. Children need and enjoy repetition.

✦ Encourage children to first join you in only the action, then in the words also. However, a young child may also "participate" by only observing you.

✦ Be enthusiastic! Use an expressive voice, face and manner while leading a finger fun activity.

Everyone's a Winner in These Games

EARLY CHILDHOOD

Games for young children involve guided play with materials that can be explored, manipulated or combined. Some activities simply foster enjoyment of the task and positive attitudes toward church. Other games may have specific Bible-related goals in addition to enjoyment and positive attitudes.

Whatever the primary purpose, children's strong need for involvement and direct experience is being met. Mentally, a child is challenged to think, recall, and sort information, responding with appropriate or creative use of materials. Socially and emotionally, children derive great satisfaction from interacting with one another in their tasks.

The Teacher's Role

Games for young children are really not games in the strictest sense of the word. They should not involve a long list of rules and restrictions. Rather, keep games with young children easy-going and noncompetitive. There are no winners or losers! A child may follow the rules for awhile, but as excitement builds the rules may simply slip away as children begin to enjoy themselves. The fun is in the doing, not in the end result of winning or losing.

Games are most effective as learning tools when they can be played in a variety of ways. For example, an enjoyable game for young children is one that involves two sets of matching cards. All cards can be placed in a mixed-up order on a flat surface. Children take turns matching cards. Or, distribute one set of cards to children. As you show the remaining cards, one at a time, children hold up matching cards. Adjust the difficulty of each game according to the age of the children.

Age-Level Characteristics

For all ages, keep rules to a minimum. Two- and three-year-olds enjoy the challenge of matching colors, simple shapes and pictures. Four- and five-year-olds are able to play board games and concentration games with a limited number of game pieces. Twos through fives find it fun to participate in movement games—tossing a beanbag into a bucket, moving in a variety of ways along a masking tape path, etc. These games can be easily adapted to the skill level of individual children.

Expect to play the games many times with children. A child learns best when he or she experiences success in the learning. And repetition helps provide that success!

How Well Do You Know Your Children?

EARLY CHILDHOOD

Instructions for Use:
- Duplicate one page per child.
- Fill in as much information as you know about each child.
- During the next few weeks, ask children the questions to which you do not yet know the answers.
- Periodically review the questions for each child, adding new insights you have gained about each one.

Child's Name

1. Briefly describe the child's home situation.

- Names of parents:

- Names of brothers and/or sisters (in order of birth):

- Other information you know about the child's home situation that will help you teach and relate to him or her.

2. What activities does the child like most? Least?

3. What skills does the child have difficulty with? (Cutting, using glue, folding, etc.)

4. Name several children the child enjoys playing with.

5. How does the child feel about coming to your class or program?

Exploring God's Wonderful World

EARLY CHILDHOOD

When young Sara pleads, "Let me see it!" she really means, "Let me feel it, touch it, shake it, put it in my mouth, rub it against my cheek and take a deep breath to find out how it smells!"

Firsthand experiences are the core of learning for young children. Exploring God's creation helps a child begin to sense the extent of God's love, His care and His wisdom. The wonder and excitement of a "hands-on" examination of God's world gives teachers many opportunities to help young children learn about God and themselves.

We cannot know all that goes on in the mind of a young child. But we do know that most learning results from the use of a child's senses—feeling, seeing, smelling, tasting and hearing. Learning begins as a sensory experience.

The Teacher's Role

A child's response to an experience often mirrors the teacher's response. For example, if the teacher at the God's Wonders area shows genuine awe when cutting open an apple to find a star pattern of seeds, then the children are likely to respond with amazement, too. Adults may know how and why a magnet attracts certain objects, but they need to awaken their dulled senses and consider anew that such wonders as magnetism, refraction of light in a prism and the ability of water to support weight are all truly God's wonders. Enjoy exploring God's wonders with children!

Part of the teacher's role is to provide words for a child. This helps him or her make sense of the experience and relate God to it. Once this relationship is made, the child is able to think about God (Jesus or the Bible verse he or she hears) in terms of a first-hand experience. Without such guidance, God's Wonders activities are of limited value.

The Learning Experiences

Young children are "here-and-now" people. When a teacher builds a bridge between what God's Word says and the child's interests, that child begins to understand that the Bible has meaning for him or her—right now! A child senses that Bible truths are not separated from life, but are a real part of it.

"Let's do it again!" is a favorite childhood expression. If children feel happy and satisfied with their learning experience, they will want to repeat it. Repetition is a necessary and natural part of a child's learning.

Some of God's Wonders activities will familiarize children with a concept they will hear later in the Bible story. For example, blowing sailboats across a shallow pan of water helps a child begin to understand what can happen to a boat in a windstorm.

39

When You Talk with a Young Child

EARLY CHILDHOOD

Those of us who work with young children often feel that children are like blotters, absorbing every word we say. Sometimes we talk from the moment the first child arrives until we tell the last child good-bye. But often a child simply tunes us out! Then, of course, the child misses hearing the very things we want him or her to learn. So it is important for us to choose our words wisely; we must learn to talk *with* a child rather than always *to* him or her.

Begin by listening. Listen to a child as if he or she were the only child in the room. Give your focused attention even though you might not understand every word. Your sincere interest in what the child says gives him or her a model to imitate. This will help that child become a better listener when it's your turn to talk.

Let the child take the lead. Every child has his or her own level of interest in what you say. Whenever you exceed that level, the child mentally flips the switch and tunes you out. When the child comes to you, he or she is showing you what his or her interests are. "Allison, I'm glad you showed me your picture. Tell me about it."

Get the child's attention before speaking. Adults waste lots of breath saying things when no one is listening. For instance, shouting across a room to a child results in confusion rather than communication. Go to the child. Bend down so your face is at his or her eye level. Speak the child's name. "Seth, you need to look at me for a moment. That's right. Seth, it's time for you to put your dishes in this cupboard."

Phrase comments in positive terms. "Patrick, blocks are for building, not for throwing."

Say the most important words first. After you've spoken the child's name, *briefly* state what action you want the child to do. Then you may add a reason. "Matthew, you may feed the turtle now. I think he is hungry."

Use simple words and a natural tone of voice. Speak slowly and distinctly in a soft, yet audible tone. Let your voice express your enthusiasm and interest. Add a smile to your words. Avoid baby talk or "gushing."

Use specific words. General terms leave a child confused, not knowing exactly what you mean. Rather than, "Put the toys away," say, "Alex, your red truck needs to go here on this shelf."

Tie words to experience. Understanding comes when a child hears words at the same time he or she sees the words demonstrated. Show a child the appropriate action as you describe it. For example, "Eric, this is the way to rub the picture so your sticker will stick." Eric understands immediately.

Relate the child's activity to the lesson focus. Keep in mind the lesson focus and Bible verse for each lesson. Then your natural conversation can tie children's activities and thoughts to the lesson's Bible truths. Briefly telling parts of the Bible story can also help make the connection.

For example, while children are building with blocks during a session aimed at increasing awareness of God's love and care, say, "Kyle, I like the way you are building. You're using your strong arms to lift those big blocks. God made your strong arms, Kyle." Open your Bible and say, "Our Bible says, *God cares about you!*"

Make a clear distinction between times when a child may and may not have a choice. Ask a question or offer a choice only when you are willing to let the child have an alternative. When his or her obedience is necessary, make a direct statement to that effect, assuming cooperation. Questions such as, "Colin, will you put away your truck?" leave the door wide open for an honest, "No," which then needs to be respected. A positive statement such as "Colin, you need to put away your truck," lets Colin know you mean business

GUIDED CONVERSATION

When You Talk with a Young Child

(Continued.)

and he has no choice. A middle ground approach is possible through questions that focus the child's attention on the situation but leave him free to determine the action. "Colin, it is time for our snack. What do you need to do with your truck?" Or, "Colin, would you like to roll your truck or carry your truck to the shelf?"

Avoid shaming a child. Sarcasm and ridicule have no place with young, sensitive children. Remember that children take your words literally. Their idea of humor is not the same as an adult's. Often adult attempts at humor result in hurt feelings. When a child makes a mistake, he or she most needs your words of encouragement. First, describe what you see. "Ashley, you seem unhappy because the juice spilled." Then offer a solution or let the child choose how to help. "We could use paper towels or the sponge to clean it up."

Show children the same courtesies you would adults. A child is a real person with real feelings! These feelings are important to him or her. When we rudely interrupt a child's activity and conversation, we are showing our lack of consideration for that child. We are also modeling the kind of behavior we do not want imitated! Ask yourself before you speak or act, *Would I say that to a grown-up friend? How would I interrupt another adult?* Then go to the child. "Adam, you are working very hard on your picture. You may draw one more thing on it and then it will be time to clean up."

The conversation ideas in your curriculum have been planned as conversation "starters"—words and suggestions to spark your own imagination as you guide children's thoughts and activity. Adapt this suggested conversation to fit the particular interests and needs of individual children. Be alert and sensitive to each child. "How good is a timely word!" (Proverbs 15:23, *NIV*).

Ways to Get a Child's Attention

1. "Danny, it's my turn to talk and your turn to listen."

2. "I'll give stickers to the children who are sitting quietly at the table."

3. "I see Nicholas waiting quietly for his turn to talk."

4. "If you see someone helping in this picture, put your hand on your knee."

5. "You've had a turn to talk, Megan. Now it's Brandon's turn."

6. (Whispering) "I'm going to whisper a question. Whisper your answer to me."

Let's Pretend We're at Home

EARLY CHILDHOOD

The Home Living area of your classroom is a place where children can re-create what they know best—their world of family, home and friends.

The Teacher's Role

Home experiences provide a natural setting where a teacher can relate Bible truths to the children's interests and experiences. For example, in a lesson focused on responding to God's love by thanking Him for His care, the teacher at the Home Living area might say, "Let's pretend it's bedtime for the children in this family. What do you do when your mom or dad says, 'Time for bed'?"

Each child at the Home Living area is familiar with bedtime routines and eagerly begins to relive his or her experiences. Dolls, pajamas, towel, soap, Bible storybook, doll bed and blankets enhance the experience. As play continues, the teacher steps back and becomes an observer. After bedtime activities are completed she says, "Do you think your little girl would like to hear a Bible story? Here is a storybook for you

to show her." The teacher also encourages children to share bedtime prayers but does not insist, remaining sensitive to each child's home situation. "We can thank God. We can say, 'Thank You, God, for loving me.'"

As opportunities come, the teacher asks, "Does God care about us only in the daytime?

Only at night? God cares about us *all* the time. Our Bible says *God cares about you*, Ashley, every day and every night. I'm glad, aren't you?"

The everyday situations played out at the Home Living area also allow children to practice concepts such as sharing, helping, taking turns and being kind. "Let's pretend visitors are coming to our house. What do we need to get ready?" a teacher suggests during a lesson focused on helping chil-

dren show kindness. The idea of visitors is familiar to children. They respond by recounting what happens when "Carlos comes to my house to play." Actions quickly follow words.

Mr. Miller brought the materials for his Bible Learning Activity in the Home Living area—powdered juice mix, cold water, ice cubes, a pitcher, a long-handled spoon, small paper cups and napkins. "Do you think our visitors would like a drink of juice?" Mr. Miller guides children in mixing juice. Children take turns stirring. Then he suggests children invite others in the room to "visit" the Home Living family. When visitors arrive, the "hosts" offer them chairs and a small cup of juice.

Mr. Miller reinforces these demonstrations of kindness. "I see boys and girls showing kindness in this family! They know our Bible says, *Be kind to everyone.*" After the visitors leave, Mr. Miller suggests, "The people in this family know about cleaning up. Everyone in this family helps. Helping is a way to be kind, just as our Bible tells us."

Suppose the children at the Home Living area completely ignore your enthusiastic suggestions. No problem! Remain alert to children's activity. Then watch for an opportunity to relate the lesson aims and Bible verse to their actions. Basic scriptural concepts, such as God's love and care, thankfulness and showing love can easily be woven into almost

Let's Pretend
We're at Home

(Continued.)

any situation children play out.

In addition to guiding activity and conversation at the Home Living area, the assigned teacher is a listener and observer. The child's actions reveal clues to many things. Through watching and listening, a teacher learns about each child's interests, abilities, self-concept and his or her understanding of what is being taught.

Age-level Characteristics

A child's interest and activity at the Home Living area is determined by his or her level of development. Most children under three may be content to simply rock the baby, feed the baby or put the baby to bed. They may want to *be* the baby, sitting in the high chair or lying in the doll bed. These youngest children in your group play alongside other children, but rarely involve anyone else in their activity. Since their command of words is limited, they often use play as a means of expressing ideas.

During the years of three, four and five, the child becomes more verbal and play becomes more complex. He or she spends additional time at play and needs extra "props" such as dress-up clothes and accessories. As children mature, they learn to interact with other children and adopt roles to become a "family."

Teaching Bible Truths to Young Children

EARLY CHILDHOOD

Guiding children in their early years is an awesome task. Helping children learn basic scriptural truth is extremely important. Fortunately, God has not left us to accomplish this task in our own strength. He offers us the instruction of the Holy Spirit and the promise of His guidance: "If any of you lacks wisdom, he should ask God, who gives generously to all" (James 1:5, *NIV*).

With this assurance of guidance, how does one go about teaching little ones of God's love? How do we communicate Bible truth in terms a child can understand?

Learning by Doing

The Christianity we share with children must be more than mere words or knowledge. It is not enough for the young child to hear God's Word or even to memorize it. The child must *do* it. Hands-on activity is the young child's most effective way to learn. He or she is not yet able to play with ideas; the child must play with *materials*. The child must use all of his or her senses—seeing, touching, tasting, smelling and hearing—in order to learn effectively. Therefore, we must help the child learn Bible truths through active play experiences. As the child draws or builds with blocks or tucks a doll into bed, a teacher can link those activities to Bible words and events, creating an effective learning experience out of what may seem to be "just play."

For instance in a simple beanbag game, reinforce Bible learning with questions and comments like these: "Ashley, you tossed the

> *Hands-on activity is the young child's most effective way to learn.*

beanbag into the basket! I remember when you were too little to do that. Now you've grown taller and stronger, just as God planned. You are even big enough to learn ways to be kind to others. You are big enough to take turns tossing the beanbag. Taking turns is a way to be kind. Our Bible says, 'Be kind to one another.'"

> *Teaching methods are only effective when the love of the teacher shines through.*

Attitude and Commitment

The best teaching methods, however, are only effective when the love and Christian commitment of the teacher shine through. Do you realize how much Jesus loves little ones? Do you want to share God's love with children to help them make a good beginning? The answers to those questions have nothing to do with size, finances, programs or facilities. They are questions about attitude and commitment. Help for changing attitudes and creating commitment can come only through earnest prayer.

Three stonemasons, when asked what they were doing, replied as follows:

"Laying a stone,"
said the first.
"Making a wall,"
said the second.
"Building a cathedral,"
said the third.

Three Sunday School teachers were asked what they were doing:

"Baby-sitting these kids,"
said the first.
"Caring for the children,"
said the second.
"Sharing God's love,"
replied the third.

Your vision of what God is doing through you can recharge your enthusiasm and change your attitude! Ask God to give you that vision.

Strike a Chord with Music

EARLY CHILDHOOD

"Let's pretend we are trees. Today a very gentle wind is blowing us," the teacher says as she fastens her hands together over her head. The children imitate her actions as she sings (to "Mulberry Bush" tune),

> "This is the way
> the trees are bending,
> Trees are bending,
> trees are bending.
> This is the way
> the trees are bending
> In the gentle wind."

Teacher and children sway gently as they sing. Then she says, "Now a big, *strong* wind is blowing!" And she sings,

> "This is the way
> the trees are bending,
> Trees are bending,
> trees are bending,
> This is the way
> the trees are bending
> In the big strong wind."

This time the "trees" bend over and back in the "strong wind."

"That big, *strong* wind almost blew us over!" comments the teacher as she and the children repeat the song and actions.

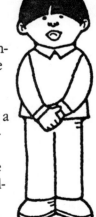

This song, which the teacher began without any "Now-we-will-sing" kind of announcement helps children build an understanding for the Bible story of Jesus calming the storm which the children will hear later in the session. The song introduces them to the difference between a gentle and a strong wind. The physical activity helps them feel what could happen in such winds. The teacher *used* the song for a definite purpose.

In planning music for young children, the key word is *use*. Music is a teaching tool to be *used* for accomplishing a specific Bible learning aim. Instead of asking children, "What do you want to sing?" select each song with a definite purpose in view.

As you use the songs in your curriculum, keep in mind the following:

Songs can teach a Bible truth. As the leader and children sing about God's loving care, the fact of God's love and care for each child becomes imprinted on young hearts and minds. Each week as a child sings God's Word, those words become a part of his or her understanding. Words sung have a deeper impression than words spoken!

Songs can relate God's Word to a child's everyday experience. Children are here-and-now people. They need to see clearly that God's Word speaks to their current situation. A song about family members, for example, gives children opportunities to tell, then sing about the people God made to love and care for them.

Songs can help establish friendly feelings at church. As children gather for group activities, the leader sings,

> "Eric's here; Sara's here.
> We're glad we are together.
> Marta's here; Jason's here.
> We're here in (sunny) weather."

Hearing his or her own name helps each child feel he or she is an important part of the group. The song also helps children learn each other's names.

Songs can provide meaningful activity. After children have become familiar with a song asking children to suggest actions, the leader asks, "Can you think of something to do with your feet that we can all do with you?" When a volunteer responds, the leader and children act on the child's suggestion. What a boost to a child's self-esteem when an adult uses his or her idea in the song!

Songs can guide activity. For example, when it's time to put away toys, the leader (or a teacher) may sing a cleanup song several times. The words to this type of song direct children in putting

EARLY CHILDHOOD

MUSIC

Strike a Chord with Music

(Continued.)

away Bible Learning Activity materials and equipment. The song is open-ended—structured so the leader can sing about specific cleanup activities (e.g., "Let's put the blocks away...").

Music does sound like an effective way to teach Bible truths to young children, but I don't read music. I can't even sing very well and we have no one to play the piano, you may be saying. Don't worry! Even the most unmusical teacher can use songs successfully. Many of the songs in your curriculum are sung to a familiar, easy-to-sing melody—usually a folk tune or a traditional song.

Remember, you are *not* performing or providing entertainment. You are *using* a song to guide children in growing awareness of God's love and care within the everyday world of family, home, friends and church. Your musical perfection is unimportant. However, your enthusiasm and interest are vital! Be willing to make mistakes. If you forget the tune, keep going with the words. Children will be delighted that you, too, are learning. Relax and enjoy the children's response to the songs. When you truly sing from a heart of love for the Lord, children are quick to catch your feeling of joy.

Making Choices—A Skill Every Child Needs

EARLY CHILDHOOD

"Welcome, Brian! I'm so glad you came to Sunday School today. Find your place at one of the tables. Later, I'll tell you what you need to know, what you should do and how you should do it."

Doesn't this sound like a simple, uncomplicated way to teach young children?

Simple? Uncomplicated? Yes, but ineffective if we want to reach our goal of meaningful Bible learning.

Instead of expecting children to be passive receivers of information, we should help each child make choices as an active learner. Never forget that children learn by doing.

Making choices helps a child develop a sense of independence—not independence to the exclusion of authority and direction, but independence that allows the child to make good choices. Never allowing a child to make a choice can be harmful, now and in the years to come.

> *Allowing children to make choices will help you avoid discipline problems.*

If a child is always looking for someone else to make decisions, he or she can become a pawn for any strong authority figure to lead astray.

Making small choices, such as which color crayon to use or whether to work in the Block area or in the Home Living corner, can actually help prepare a young child to make life's larger decisions. Because the child eventually must "Choose...this day whom you will serve" (Joshua 24:15, *NIV*), we must help children develop wise choice-making skills. The child who is rarely allowed to make decisions may find it harder to make the ultimate decision of responding to Jesus Christ.

A child develops a sense of responsibility through making choices. A responsible person is one who makes a choice after having fully considered the consequences of that choice. Learning to be accountable for choices made will help the child in making responsible choices.

Allowing children to make some of their own choices will help you avoid discipline problems. Children's behavior is more positive when they are doing something they have chosen. In contrast, when a child is told to do something he or she doesn't want to do, he or she becomes unhappy and usually will let everyone know it.

Allowing a child to make choices tells the child you believe he or she is capable of making a decision. Your trust is an essential foundation for a child's healthy development.

Prayer and the Young Child

EARLY CHILDHOOD

Prayer can be a meaningful form of worship for a young child. Unfortunately, it sometimes is done in ways that make it the most boring. What are some ways we can help young children grow in their desire and ability to express themselves to God?

First, let's examine what young children can understand about prayer.

1. God wants us to talk to Him, and He hears us.

2. We can pray anytime, anywhere—not only in Sunday School and church, but in our homes, at school, in the car and at the store, etc.

3. We can pray silently, aloud or by singing.

4. Closing our eyes helps us think of what we are talking about instead of thinking about other things.

> *Short, specific prayers teach that prayer deals with things of interest to the child.*

Following are some guidelines to assist you in teaching these facts to young children.

1. The way *you* pray shows that prayer is important in your own life. Your example shows what prayer is. If you pray long, adult-level prayers, you are teaching children that prayer is for grown-ups and is very complicated. However, if you pray short, simple, specific prayers that are within the child's capacity to offer, you are teaching that prayer is simple and deals with things of interest to the child.

2. Provide prayer opportunities throughout the session. During Bible Learning Activity time, you'll discover many natural opportunities to guide a child in brief prayer. For example, when telling children about the shepherds thanking God for sending Jesus, say, "Let's thank God for sending His Son, Jesus. Dear God, thank You for sending Jesus. In Jesus' name, amen." Or as a child works with his or her hands (cutting, drawing, painting, etc.) say, "Jenae, look at the work your hands can do! God made your hands so you can hold a crayon. What other things can you do with your hands? Let's thank God for your hands. Thank You, God, for Jenae's hands. In Jesus' name, amen."

3. Encourage children to repeat short prayers after you. This experience is the first step toward the child's using his or her own words in prayer. Keep the prayer short and use simple words that are clear to the child. For a prayer to be meaningful, a child should understand what he or she is saying or what is being said.

4. Prayers need not always be spoken. Many songs are prayers in themselves. Ask children to listen carefully as you read aloud the words of the song. Point out that the prayer song is addressed to God. Encourage children to close their eyes while they sing.

Young children can know that the Lord's Prayer is a prayer Jesus taught and that it is recorded in our Bible. However, the phrases are long and many of the words are symbolic and beyond the understanding of a young child. When he or she is older, memorizing this significant passage of Scripture will be a more meaningful experience than during those early years.

A child needs to hear teachers pray often. A teacher's attitude of reverence and sincerity is keenly felt by a child. Our task is to earnestly communicate to children the importance of prayer. God's Spirit working through us and His Word will help us in this task.

Remember: The most meaningful and trustworthy method of teaching children to pray is your example. Talking to God about things within the child's experience will increase his or her understanding about prayer.

51

I've Got Rhythm

EARLY CHILDHOOD

Everyone who spends much time with young children knows the enduring popularity of nursery rhymes and the universal tendency of children to create rhythmic chants which accompany their play. Words which have a rhythmic pattern are easy to remember. And words that are remembered can powerfully influence understanding and attitudes. With or without a melody, rhythm adds impact to the words we want children to learn.

Because children respond to rhythm, any teacher can easily increase children's ability to learn and remember Bible verses by presenting them in simple rhythmic patterns. For example: "Do not forget to share with others" (Hebrews 13:16, *NIV*) can be chanted as:

"Do NOT forGET to
SHARE with OTHers,"

or as:

"Do not forGET to
share with OTHers."

Also,

"The Lord has done
great things"
(Psalm 126:3, *NIV*)

can be chanted as:

"The LORD (pause)
has done great things,"

or as:

"The LORD has DONE
great THINGS."

Most Bible verses can also be sung to simple melodies. For example, Hebrews 13:16 (above) can be sung to "Happy Birthday":

"Do not forget to share,
Do not forget to share,
Do not forget to sha-are,
To sha-are with others."

Or how about singing Psalm 126:3 to "The Farmer in the Dell"?

"The Lord has done
great things,
The Lord has done
great things."
The Bible tells me
what God does.
"The Lord has
done great things."

Rhythms/Music as a Bible Learning Activity

At its simplest, a Rhythms/Music activity needs no equipment or supplies other than an enthusiastic teacher. Begin with a simple chant which includes the child's name: "Hello, hello, I'm glad you came. Hello, hello, (Fernando's) your name." Children will enjoy learning and practicing a finger fun poem suggested in your curriculum. Then introduce them to the day's Bible verse and lead them in one or more ways of saying it as a chant.

The fun of rhythmic and musical chants can be enhanced by using "body percussion." Clapping hands (C), tapping feet (T), slapping knees (S), patting thighs (P) are easy ways to include simple movement and interesting sounds along with a chant. For example, one pattern could be:

"The LORD (C/C) has DONE (T/T) great THINGS (S/S)."

Extend interest by using simple rhythm instruments in time with the meter of the verse.

Rhythms/Music as Part of Other Activities

Just as children enjoy chanting while jumping rope and bouncing balls, they enjoy hearing and saying simple chants while drawing, building, or participating in any other learning activity. Once teachers begin using poems or songs during other experiences, children will quickly begin to do the same, significantly enriching their enjoyment and learning.

The Teacher's Role

First, spend some time before class learning and practicing the poem or song. Then, during class, simply invite children to listen once before they join in. After children have "caught on," invite them to suggest variations in the

I've Got Rhythm

(Continued.)

rhythm. Intersperse the rhythms with brief conversation about the meaning of the verse: "I'm glad the Bible tells us about the great things God has done. Giving us ears to hear and hands to clap are some of the great things the Lord has done for us."

When using rhythm instruments, give clear directions for their use and consistently enforce the instructions. If children are unable to control the impulse (often irresistible) to bang away regardless of the rhythm pattern, gently collect the instruments and repeat the instructions before allowing them to try again. (Occasionally allow children the freedom to bang and clang in accompaniment to recorded music.)

Age-Level Characteristics

Expect most two-year-olds and many younger threes to simply enjoy watching and listening as you and other children chant or sing together. Some children may begin to mimic the movements before they try joining in on the words. This typical behavior demonstrates how a child's physical abilities tend to precede the growth of verbal skills.

Once children become confident in saying or singing the words, the next major milestone occurs when they are able to suggest variations in the rhythm patterns or new words for the poem or song.

Leading a Young Child to Christ

EARLY CHILDHOOD

Most young children can understand that Jesus is always their Friend and Helper. The plan of salvation in Jesus Christ is simple and clear enough that some of these children can understand it and respond to it at their level of childlike faith (particularly those who receive Christian nurture at home).

A teacher of young children has a God-given opportunity and responsibility to nurture a child's understanding of salvation. You may be the first person in a child's life to explain these spiritual truths to him or her. Keep in mind, however, that spiritual birth, like physical birth, is part of a process. A baby must develop in the womb before birth. Jesus compared the preparation of the heart to the planting of seed which later bears fruit. Ideas and attitudes that take root in the child early in life will produce a rich harvest in years that follow.

> *Unless God is speaking to the child, there can be no genuine heart experience.*

Most conversions among children are recorded between the ages of 10 and 12. However, the child who attends Sunday School during the early years—particularly if from a supportive Christian home—often is capable of an earlier, meaningful response to Jesus' love. All children, no matter what their backgrounds, need Christian nurture to develop a personal faith.

Parents and teachers alike must be sensitive to the guidance of the Holy Spirit in leading a young child to Christ, for unless God Himself is speaking through His Spirit to the child, there can be no genuine heart experience. Parents and teachers also have the responsibility to ask questions that will show the degree of understanding the child has about salvation, plus the level of commitment he or she has to that belief. (Avoid asking leading questions or questions that can be answered yes or no.)

Your prayers for the Holy Spirit's guidance, along with your wise use of the following principles will have far-reaching results in the lives of the children you teach, including those you are preparing for an encounter with Jesus at a later stage of development.

1. Be clear about what a child needs to know to realize the basic significance of Christ's death and resurrection. It must be simple—yet complete.
  a. God loves you.
  b. You have done wrong things (sinned).
  c. God says that sin must be punished.
  d. God sent Jesus to take the punishment for your sin.
  e. Tell God you have sinned and want to stop doing wrong things.
  f. Ask Jesus to be your Savior.
  g. Then you are a member of God's family.

2. Be familiar with key Scripture passages. God's Word is powerful. Use the Bible in sharing salvation's message with children. Mark these key verses: John 3:16; Romans 3:23; 5:6; 1 Corinthians 15:3; 1 John 4:14. Use the simplest, clearest version you have available.

3. Avoid symbolism. Use words whose meanings are clear to a child. Phrases such as "born again" or "asking Jesus into your heart" are meaningful to adults, but they create misconceptions in children's minds.

(Continued.)

EARLY CHILDHOOD

SALVATION

Leading a Young Child to Christ

(Continued.)

4. Explain key terms to children to lay the foundation for acceptance into God's family. For example, briefly explain these terms: sin—doing wrong things or disobeying God's rules; saved—to become a part of God's family; forgive—to take away the punishment for doing wrong; everlasting life—to live now and forever with Jesus.

5. Talk individually to a child who expresses interest in becoming a member of God's family. Something as important as a child's personal relationship with Jesus Christ can be handled more effectively alone than in a group.

6. Allow for free choice. A child needs to respond individually to the call of God's love. This response needs to be a genuine response to God—not because the child wants to please peers, parents or you, the teacher. Be willing to allow the Holy Spirit to work within the child. A child may come to you for information, not necessarily to make a decision. Allow the Holy Spirit to lead; don't feel that a child must "do something." Be a faithful planter of the seeds of God's truth.

7. Focus on God's love and forgiveness. Let the child know there will still be times when he or she does wrong things. Remind him or her that God doesn't stop loving us when we sin. If we are sorry for the wrong things we do, God will forgive us.

Making the Sunday School Schedule Work for You

EARLY CHILDHOOD

For each child that crosses your threshold, Sunday School begins the moment he or she steps inside the door. The child's presence means, "Ready or not, here I come!" and teachers had better be ready! Thus, Sunday School begins for the staff *before* the first child arrives. The first few minutes of each child's morning in your room need to be a time of warm, personal attention from a teacher. You won't be able to provide this essential touch unless you have done all your preparing and organizing ahead of time.

What is the scene in your room when the first child appears at the door? It should look like this: All equipment and materials to be used in this session are in place where children can see them and reach them easily; a department leader or teacher is ready to welcome each child personally; other teachers are in separate activity areas, prepared to help children learn. (A department should offer one activity per teacher.)

1. Bible Learning Activity Time

Here comes the first child! The leader or teacher stoops or squats down to the child's eye level to welcome him by name. "Justin, I'm so glad to see you. We have lots of things for you to do today!" After a friendly but brief word to the parents, Justin is brought into the room. He may need a bit of help with his coat. However, let the child do as much for himself as possible. Justin finds his own name tag. If he has brought an offering,

guide him to visit the offering center and say, "We bring our money because we love God." Justin is now ready to choose the activity he wants to participate in first. Make suggestions when needed, but do not force a child to participate against his or her will.

As the other children arrive, the procedure is repeated. Teachers remain at their assigned areas whether or not children have begun working at that activity.

If a child arrives BEFORE all teachers are ready, provide one or more skill toys (puzzles, construction toys, etc.) until the staff is ready to begin the lesson activities.

Why begin with a choice of activities? There are several reasons. First, children do not all arrive at the same time. If the session began with large group time, the constant interruption of children and teachers arriving would greatly distract the group's attention.

Second, few children come to Sunday School mentally and physically ready to sit quietly. It's too early in the day for that! They are filled with energy and vitality; they want something to do! Bible Learning Activities provide a purposeful means of releasing this energy.

Third, the activities that teachers provide are designed to capture children's interest and to naturally guide their thinking to the lesson focus for the day. For example, as a child begins playing with play dough, the teacher at that table may say, "It's fun to play with play dough. Look what you can do with your hands. God made our hands."

Fourth, even young children

prefer to make their own choices. A multitude of discipline problems can be avoided by allowing children to select from among several possibilities, rather than telling them to do what everyone else is doing. Giving children a choice helps them learn to make decisions and to accept responsibility. It also shows that you have respect for them. Children work harder and learn more at an activity they have chosen.

Throughout Bible Learning Activity Time, children are allowed to move freely to whatever activity they desire. Participation in an activity should only be limited by the space available at the activity area. When children tire of one activity, they move to another. This freedom of movement creates a relaxed atmosphere that both teachers and children enjoy.

Some observers ask, "When do the children stop playing and start learning?" Play IS the way God planned for young children to do most of their learning. As children engage in building with blocks, sorting toys by color, playing out experiences in the Home Living area, they are learning how to relate to other children. They are discovering that church people are concerned about important things in life. Resist the temptation to chat with other teachers during this time. Your participation in action and word is essential to effective Bible Learning Activities. As a teacher casually asks questions and engages children in conversation, they are led to begin thinking about the lesson concepts for that

EARLY CHILDHOOD

Making the Sunday School Schedule Work for You

(Continued.)

morning. And often there are many opportunities to spontaneously share a Bible verse, sing a song or tell the Bible story. Because this firsthand learning is so important to young children, at least half of the Sunday School session is spent in these activities.

During this time of small group activities, if a department leader is available, he or she may move from group to group, quietly assisting where needed. Behavior problems, such as crying children, can be handled by the leader, thus allowing teachers to focus on the group in their area. If it is necessary for the leader to guide an activity, he or she should still be alert to any later arrivers or potential behavior problems which may need attention.

Bible Learning Activity Time concludes when the leader indicates with a signal, such as by singing a song, that it is time to clean up. Children learn responsibility and the importance of helping when they participate in cleanup. The children come to the Together Time area as they complete cleanup tasks. The leader or a teacher begins to lead activity songs or finger fun as the first few children gather.

2. Together Time

The second major time block in the schedule brings all the children and teachers together in a semicircle on the rug. This time spent in a large group helps the leader develop and express a group feeling of unity and concern. Assume that children will join activities. Identify children who are respond-

ing positively. Other children will be drawn by this attention.

Simple games and songs help children become aware of each other. When the leader begins to sing, "I have a good friend, (Nicole) is her name," attention is focused on individual children and teachers in the group. By asking the group, "Who is not here today?" or leading them in prayer for a child who is ill, the leader builds a concern for others.

Bringing everyone together provides opportunities for the leader to reinforce the Bible learning that took place during Bible Learning Activity Time. Conversation, songs, finger fun, sharing a Bible Learning Activity, and prayer all call attention to the lesson focus.

The large group time includes a variety of experiences which change the pace of the morning. Children will tire less readily when they are given a balance of active and quiet things to do. If children get restless during conversation about a picture, for example, lead the group in an active song. Doing something new always sparks interest. When children are quietly interested in what is going on, invite them to a moment of prayer.

3. Bible Story Time

Our objective in telling Bible stories to small children is not primarily for them to remember the details of the events. It is to allow the biblical material to reveal God's involvement in the everyday business of living.

The Bible story may be told in a large group or in small groups. If you have more than eight or ten

children and two or more teachers, you may divide the class into at least two Bible story groups that meet with a teacher in different parts of the room. If the story is told in the large group, divide into groups to complete the Activity Page after the story is finished.

The groups sit around a table or form a small circle on the floor. Each teacher leads a group in completing the Activity Page. These are permanently assigned groups of no more than four to six children. This arrangement allows children to identify closely with one particular teacher. Children need this sense of added security. In these small groups there is ample opportunity for personal interaction between teacher and children.

4. Song and Fun Time

As soon as one or two children complete the Activity Page, Song and Fun Time begins. This provides a smooth transition to the second hour program or until parents arrive. The leader or a teacher guides children in activity songs, finger fun and simple games. Children need this opportunity to stretch their muscles and to enjoy a change of pace.

Teachers may either participate in the large group activities, or welcome new arrivals and assist those children who leave with their parents. Keep the door to your room closed to prevent children from leaving without an adult. Parents should wait outside the room while a teacher brings their child to the door.

Sharing Can Be Fun

EARLY CHILDHOOD

"I want that truck!" demands a child.

"No, I had it first!" shouts another.

A teacher approaches saying, "Why don't you take turns with the truck?"

To adults, taking turns or sharing means cooperation and equal participation. But it has a far different meaning to a child. To young children, taking turns means one child has to give up something, with the possibility of being left with nothing in its place. To the child, it doesn't seem fair! Yet sharing is important and necessary for children to learn. We need to give children opportunities to work together to learn cooperation. Provide chances to share in as many class activities as possible. Bible Learning Activity Time offers excellent situations to encourage children to work together.

Having a box of crayons, a pair of scissors and a bottle of glue for each child at the **ART** table will not encourage children to work together. Instead, provide

two or three of these items to be shared by four to six children. Large-scale art activities such as murals and collages help children learn to work side by side. While each child's contribution will be unique, the child will enjoy feeling like part of a group effort.

BLOCK activities give children many ways to learn about working together. Initially, a teacher may need to build with children, demonstrating "taking turns" by adding a block to the structure and sharing the blocks. Eventually the teacher can withdraw from the activity, but should stay nearby to encourage children to continue building cooperatively. Children may help each other build a church, an airport, houses and towers. As children work, the teacher's conversation will give children ideas for ways to cooperate as they build. For example, "Luis, Tim needs a long block for the house. How can you help him?" The children will gradually learn ways to cooperate with each other.

In the **BOOK** area, one child may hold a book and turn pages while another child tells about the pictures. Or, one child holds the book while the other turns pages. Children take turns telling about the pictures. A teacher will need to be nearby to involve children in this activity.

A similar sharing of activities can be encouraged in the **SKILL TOYS** activities. Provide half as many puzzles (or pegboards, beads, etc.) as there are children. Encourage children to work together by taking turns placing puzzle pieces.

Many games require children to work together. A teacher's conversation can help children work WELL together. "I see you are waiting your turn," and "Brendan, thank you for helping Nina count out three cards" are comments that will encourage children to work cooperatively. Since young children live in the immediate moment, waiting for others is one of the most difficult tasks in working together. (Keep your expectations about sharing realistic. It is easier for a child to wait patiently when there are only four or five in a game, rather than ten. Do not expect the young child to wait patiently while ten others are taking their turns.) It is also important to give clear directions for a game. Sometimes children's uncooperative behavior is caused by their lack of understanding about what they are to do.

GOD'S WONDERS activities provide opportunities for children to work together to learn about God's world. Children may help each other care for a pet or plants and work together to collect items for a display table. Children can patiently wait their turn to place an item in a dishpan of water to see if it sinks or floats, or wait to

feel in a sack to discover one of God's Wonders.

As in every home, there are many opportunities for children to work together in the **HOME LIVING** area. Encourage activities such as cleaning house or preparing a pretend meal or a real snack. Such shared tasks enable children to have fun while learning ways to help each other.

Give children opportunities to make decisions about how they work together. Deciding who will be the mommy (or daddy), who will play with which doll and who will put forks on the table all teach children how to work well together. A teacher should be nearby to help when those decisions get a bit sticky. "Sue, you've been the mommy already today. It's Jill's turn."

RHYTHMS activities help children learn to work together in ways that please them immediately. Children singing and playing instruments quickly learn that being together is fun. They enjoy making new verses. It's encouraging for a child to hear everyone singing words he or she suggested. They can pass rhythm instruments around the group so that everyone gets to play each of the instruments.

Children can learn that sharing means cooperation, not sacrifice. Turn squabbles into opportunities to learn new ways to share. Sharing results in fun, uninterrupted play and learning.

Folding, Taping, Gluing and Cutting

EARLY CHILDHOOD

To help children successfully complete some of the activities suggested in your curriculum, a few basic skills are required. These skills—folding, taping, cutting and gluing—must be learned. And as you know, not all children learn at the same rate. There are a variety of ways to help children learn to succeed at these four tasks. Some of these ways are listed below.

Folding

1. Before giving paper to child, prefold paper as needed, then open it back up. Paper will then fold easily along the prefolded lines when child refolds it.

2. Score the line to be folded by placing a ruler on the line. Then draw a used ball-point pen with no ink in it along the ruler's edge. The line will fold easily into place.

3. Hold the corners of the paper in position to be folded. Tell the child to "press and rub" where he or she wants to fold it.

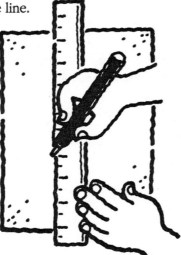

Taping

1. An easy solution for the problems of taping is to use double-sided tape whenever appropriate. Lay the tape down on the paper where it is needed. Child attaches the item that needs to be taped.

2. If double-sided tape is not available or is not appropriate, place a piece of tape lightly on the page where indicated. Child rubs on tape to attach it securely to paper.

Gluing

1. Have child use a glue bottle to apply a spot of glue to a large sheet of paper, then he or she presses a smaller piece of paper onto glued area.

2. Provide a glue stick for the child to use (available at variety stores). Take off cap and roll up glue for child. Child "colors" with glue stick over desired area.

3. Pour glue into a shallow container. Thin slightly by adding a small amount of water. Child uses paintbrush to spread glue over desired area. This idea works well when a large surface needs to be glued.

4. To glue a smaller surface, pour a small amount of glue into a shallow container. Give each child a cotton swab. Child dips the swab into the glue and rubs on desired area.

5. When using glue bottles, buy the smallest bottles for children to use. Refill small bottles from a large bottle. (a) Adjust top to limit amount of glue that comes out. (b) Instruct child to put "tiny dots of glue" on paper. (c) Clean off and tightly close top of bottle when finished.

(Continued.)

Cutting

1. Cutting with scissors is one of the most difficult tasks for any young child to master. Consider purchasing several pairs of "training scissors" (available at educational supply stores) to assist in teaching children how to cut.

2. Have available in your classroom two or three pairs of left-handed scissors (also available at educational supply stores). All scissors should be approximately 4 inches (10 cm) long and should have blunt ends.

3. Hold paper tightly at ends or sides while child cuts.

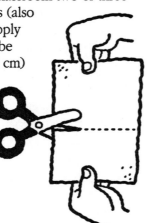

4. Begin to cut paper for child to follow. Child follows cut you have begun.

5. Draw simple lines outside actual cut lines for the child to follow. This will help a child cut close to the desired shape—though it will not be exact.

6. Provide scrap paper for the child to practice cutting.

Remember not to expect perfection. Accept all attempts at accomplishing the task. Specific and honest praise will encourage the child to attempt the task again!

Puzzles, Pegs and Patterns

EARLY CHILDHOOD

Every child comes equipped with an endless supply of wiggles, squirms and bursts of energy. Recognizing and accepting the differences in children of the same age helps the teacher to be flexible, changing and rearranging an activity to meet individual needs.

Skill toys, such as puzzles, bristle blocks, interlocking blocks, pegs and pegboards, are excellent activities for groups in which there are wide spans of ability levels. Provide skill toys that challenge children at various levels of physical maturity. Success in using a toy depends upon the child's patience, coordination and dexterity, not necessarily his or her age. For example, most children under two need puzzles with only three or four pieces. Each piece should be a picture of a whole object (cat, drum, etc.). As children

grow, they will enjoy working puzzles with more pieces which are parts of a whole object.

When you see a child becoming frustrated with a puzzle, step in with suggestions that will allow the child the satisfaction of completing the puzzle independently. "I wonder if the piece will fit if

you turn it around? This part of the puzzle is red. Can you find another red piece that will fit right here?" Acknowledge and encourage each child's efforts.

Children will be more likely to participate in this activity if you set a few pieces of the toy out on the floor or a table. Begin putting the toy together. Invite a child to start work on his or her own construction or help with what you are doing.

Skill toys help satisfy a child's desire to achieve. They provide an opportunity for a child to work alone or with one or two friends. The child learns to share and take turns. When a child works a puzzle or builds a tower with interlocking blocks, he or she learns to think, to reason and to solve problems. Working with skill toys also helps children develop eye-hand coordination and can prepare children for learning to read by helping them distinguish shapes and patterns.

Expect to begin a construction or puzzle many times during Bible Learning Activity Time. A child learns best when he or she experiences success in the learning. And repetition helps provide that success!

The Teacher's Role

The teacher has four major tasks in guiding children to use skills toys as resources which aid Bible learning:

1. Select toys which can be successfully used by the age group. For example, teachers of two- and three-year-old children should

choose puzzles with no more than eight or ten pieces, while four- and five-year-olds need the challenge of puzzles with at least 12-15 pieces. Avoid toys or puzzles with many small pieces for two-year-olds and younger threes. Select toys which offer a challenge for the older child. If you have a mixed-age group, select items which can be used safely and enjoyably by all.

2. Play with the materials yourself to stimulate children's interest. However, avoid the temptation to build elaborate creations which make the children's efforts seem inadequate. Children enjoy patterning activities with many skill toys: "I'll make a design, then you make one just like it."

3. Assist children as necessary in getting started and in successfully completing use of a toy. One effective approach is to engage

Puzzles, Pegs and Patterns

(Continued.)

the child in taking turns: "I'll put in one piece, then you put in another."

4. Guide the conversation to connect children's activity to the lesson aims: "You sure do a good job of using your hands to fit pieces together. What are some ways you use your hands at home to help others?" "I can tell you're enjoying yourself this morning. I'm glad we can be together at our church."

Age-Level Characteristics

Because most skill toys require successful eye-hand coordination, you may notice a distinct progression in children's abilities to work with these materials as they mature. In addition, expect younger children to engage in more repetitive actions (putting the same puzzle together several times, building the same shapes, etc.) than older children.

Often the child's patience and attention span develop hand-in-hand with small muscle control. The younger child is likely to

complete a few steps, dismantle what was done and start over many times, while the older child is more likely to stick with longer, more complex tasks. While these abilities are the result of maturation and experience, any two children of the same age may show markedly different levels of development. Choose materials which allow for flexible use, and be accepting of each child's present skill level.

Helping Children with Special Needs

EARLY CHILDHOOD

The Hyperactive Child

A clinically hyperactive child is different from a child who can't sit still for very long. The hyperactive child reacts to life the way you would respond to being closed in a room with the television, radio, stereo system and two vacuum cleaners all turned up full blast. Sound like too much for you? A classroom often seems like "too much" for the hyperactive child.

Hyperactive children are unable to sort out and concentrate on one thing at a time. They are in constant motion mentally and often physically as well. Since such children cannot sit and listen or even work on one project for any length of time, they leap from one distraction to another, and often distract others at the same time.

Hyperactive children need your special love and patience. Such children often need extra adult guidance and attention. Thus, it is wise to plan for an extra helper when a hyperactive child is part of a group. Look for a kind, loving person who will focus on this child's special needs.

Assist hyperactive children in choosing primarily quiet activities which help keep their energies channeled. Hyperactive children function best with a minimum of distraction and in an activity which captures their attention.

Be aware of the needs of the other children at the same time. You cannot allow one or a few children to disrupt others unnecessarily or reduce your classroom to chaos.

Talk privately and in a loving and understanding manner with parents. Get firsthand information on the most effective ways to care for their child. You will find the parents highly appreciative of your concern for the child's well-being. Since they know their child better than anyone else, they will likely be able to suggest approaches which have proven helpful.

The Shy Child

A shy child may often feel insecure and afraid. Or the child may be a natural introvert. It is important that every child feel safe and loved.

Never call a child "shy." (The child may try to live up to the label you place on him or her!) Avoid insisting that a shy child talk in a large group. Never shame a child into responding! A quiet child will usually feel more free to talk in a small group where every child is freely participating. Such a child may eventually respond in a large group after having many successful experiences in small, informal groups.

Be sure that quiet children receive your personal attention and encouragement. It's easy to overlook them. Consistently help shy children feel welcome and important without being made the focus of group attention.

The Aggressive Child

The child who most needs love and acceptance is often the one whose behavior makes others feel anything but loving! Unfortunately, a natural tendency to withhold love from such a child is likely to produce even more aggressive, unacceptable behavior as the child desperately seeks to be noticed.

As with any other child, the rule of thumb is to accept the aggressive child as he or she is, not requiring that the child change in order to earn your affection. But every time there is positive behavior, be sure the child knows you appreciate his or her efforts. Your good example of showing love to aggressive children by encouraging and affirming them will also help teach all children ways to relate to each other.

If an aggressive child upsets or harms another child, you will need to be firm but friendly. Remove the aggressive child from the situation. Clearly explain the behavior necessary in order to return to the group.

Five Steps to Becoming a Better Storyteller

EARLY CHILDHOOD

Bible story time is the focal point of every session. Unfortunately, too many teachers wind up boring young children during the Bible story time because they do not work on simple basic guidelines to good storytelling:

Guideline #1—Teach from the Bible, not your curriculum. Children need to see you as a teacher of God's Word—not merely a reader of a curriculum product. Have your open Bible in front of you throughout the story, and clearly state that the story is true: "It really happened to real people."

Guideline #2—Know your story well enough to talk *with* your students rather than read *to* them. Make simple notes to help you remember and properly sequence the three or four most important events. When your eyes are not tied to the words of the story, you are free to focus on the faces of the children in your class. By *telling* rather than *reading* the story, you will be better able to express enthusiasm through your face and voice. Knowing the story well also enables you to freely use your hands to move any Bible story figures on the flannel board.

Guideline #3—Ask good questions at the beginning and end of a story. Young children need to hear a logical flow in the story line. Since their attention is easily diverted, they need to hear a story from beginning to end without interruptions in order to understand it. Decide what you want children to focus on in the story. Ask them to listen for that before you begin telling the story (e.g., "In our story today, listen to find out what God wanted David to do.") Then at the end of the story, ask them to give you the information from the story they just heard (e.g., "What did God want David to do in our story?") Asking questions in this way helps children discover information on their own. And children will remember what they discover for themselves longer than the things they merely hear us tell them.

Guideline #4—Emphasize the main goal of the Bible story character. This element is the key to being able to recall information in the story. Clearly define the main goal of the principal character in your story. Emphasize this goal when you tell the story. By your emphasis, children's ability to recall the main goal will increase dramatically.

Guideline #5—Practice. Take time to practice telling your Bible stories out loud! Use a cassette tape recorder, practice occasionally with another teacher from your department, tell the story to a family member, or even practice storytelling in front of a mirror. Be sure that you are giving your best to God and to the children He has entrusted to you.

Ideas for Summer Sunday School

EARLY CHILDHOOD

"Where is my teacher?" asked Latasha as she came into her Sunday School room one morning in August.

"Mrs. Scott has gone on a vacation," a teacher answered.

"I like it when she's back," was Latasha's response.

Teacher, you are important to the little ones in your class. You provide a consistent security by your presence. The children miss you when you are away. Before leaving for your vacation, explain to your class that you will not be in Sunday School for several Sundays. Show a picture of a plane, car, bus or other way that you will travel. If possible, show the children a picture of a place you will be or something you will see or do while you are away.

Help children become acquainted with the teacher who will substitute for you. Tell children the name of your substitute. If possible, include your substitute in at least some part of the class period for the week before you leave. The substitute and the children will feel more comfortable if children know who their teacher will be and if the new teacher knows the basic class procedures.

As you pack for your trip, include the address of each child in your class. Mail each one a picture postcard with a short note. Send one to the class for the substitute and children to enjoy together.

Vacationing Children

It will be important to help children maintain contact with the Sunday School class during their vacations, too. Send home a note with children (or post the note on your hall bulletin board) asking parents to mail your class a picture postcard while the family is vacationing. Mention that hearing from vacationers helps children know "God loves and cares for us wherever we are." Each week display postcards and read the message aloud to children. Encourage children to tell you about the places they have been.

Vacation Treasures

Suggest vacationing teachers and children bring back something for your God's Wonders area. Each one can locate some part of God's creation, such as shells, rocks, pinecones, etc., from his or her vacation spot. Teachers and children tell something about the place they visited as they show their items.

Visitors

Vacation time will bring visiting children to your class. Remember that these young children are not accustomed to you or to your room. For some, Sunday School may be a new experience. Show the visitor equipment and materials. Do not insist that a visitor participate in every part of the schedule. Should the child become disruptive, a teacher should gently lead him or her from the group and play, read or talk quietly in another part of the room. Visitors need your patience and understanding guidance for a happy and meaningful learning experience.

Returning Children

When young children return to Sunday School from vacation, they may act like visitors. You may wish to ask a parent to stay in the room until "Sue feels happy again" in the activities she formerly enjoyed. Encourage Sue to show her parents something you remember she liked before. Talk about the object Sue brought from her vacation. If parents are embarrassed or annoyed, remind them that this often happens and Sue will adjust quickly if she again receives understanding as a newcomer.

Summer months can provide a relaxed time for growing, an appreciation of the changes of season that are a part of God's plan for our world, and a time of strengthened relationships if teachers, parents and children work together with a patient, caring attitude. Make your summer a time of refreshment and growth!

Help Children Learn to Learn

EARLY CHILDHOOD

As a teacher you come in contact with children from various backgrounds, family structures and environments. In order to provide effective lessons for all the children you teach, plan learning experiences which adapt to a wide variety of skills and abilities.

A child blooms and grows noticeably when provided with stimulating activities that use all five senses. A child who has not had a stimulating environment may struggle with tasks that other children at the same age seem to do with ease. The most common reason a child may have difficulty performing tasks or relating appropriately to other children is simply lack of experience.

A child unable to do something may: (1) *withdraw* from the activity due to embarrassment, lack of interest or shyness; (2) *watch*, but not participate in the activity; (3) *participate in the activity with extra energy*, often resulting in an incomplete task or unpleasant contact with other children; or (4) *become frustrated* when the activity is too difficult.

If you know a child cannot do a certain activity, plan a way to involve the child without undue stress. Helping the child develop skills to participate with the class is very important. With individual attention and opportunities for practice, a child can learn a variety of skills.

(Continued.)

Teaching Tip

1 *Pair the child who needs to develop a skill with another child who has mastered the skill.* Tell the child who needs to learn the activity that the two children can work together doing the same thing. Have the child watch the model and do what the model does. This technique will give the child confidence if you monitor the children and provide plenty of encouragement. A smile or even a hug may be just the thing when both children are working together and learning the task at hand.

An alternative approach is to have a teacher be the model, carefully demonstrating one step at a time.

Teaching Tip

2 *Once the child has observed the basic skills, practice is needed.* For example, the child who has trouble cutting needs to cut scrap paper to develop good coordination. Practice may be done in class or the child and parents may want to work on the activity at home. Working at home with parents is a good first step in becoming comfortable with the activity in front of peers.

Learning involves making mistakes and not being afraid to try a new activity. If the child shows signs of discouragement at completing a task, offer to take turns doing parts of the work. ("While you rest your fingers, would you like me to cut a little bit?")

Teaching Tip

3 *The very active child who has problems interacting with other children may need some additional guidance.* This child may never have participated in a group activity before. For example, if a child insists on taking all the crayons at one time, step in and quietly point out how the other children are using their crayons one at a time. Sometimes the child is afraid the crayon will be gone when he or she will need it. Reassure the child that the crayons will be there when needed.

EARLY CHILDHOOD

Teaching Tip

4 *Praise every good effort as often as possible.* For example, by praising those who share their crayons, you will help children remember the value of sharing week after week. Acknowledging a child doing something right is important, but DO NOT make a child feel inadequate by pointing out negative comparisons ("Johnny is doing this right, but you're not!" is a damaging rebuke to any child.).

Teaching Tip

5 *Whenever you help children who are unfamiliar with a task or activity, break down the task into simpler steps.* By letting the child learn one part at a time, you increase the potential for success. Learning is easier in smaller steps. This method works in groups as well as individually. Children cannot remember many directions at one time. They are much more likely to succeed when one task is presented and completed before another new one is begun.

Teaching new material in small, easy steps may be used with any activity you plan for your children. Whether the activities involve acting out a story, using scissors, or working or playing in a group, break tasks down so each child can learn new skills and feel successful.

When you take the time to observe what your children can do, you will be ready to help them grow and learn. Making the effort to affirm them for their efforts and their progress will encourage maximum growth. "How good is a timely word!" (Proverbs 15:23, *NIV*). Children who receive encouragement will be motivated to continue learning.

Notes

EARLY CHILDHOOD

Making the Connection with Today's Kids

How can a book written for adults centuries ago in a vastly different culture possibly have meaning for today's young child? How can we use this guidebook of our faith to introduce a child to biblical principles?

We tell Bible stories and teach Bible verses, for in them we learn timeless truths about God and His Son, the Lord Jesus. The portions of God's Word we share with children deal with basic human needs which are the same for all persons, regardless of age, geographic location or cultural setting. For example, today, as in Abraham's time, all of us need to grow in trusting God and obeying Him.

Bible Stories

Bible truths impact the mind, feelings and behavior of a young child when those truths relate directly to the child's world. When the situations of the Bible story characters are similar to situations children have already encountered, children will be more likely to connect the example to their own world. For a story to be effective in capturing interest and stimulating learning, children should be able to identify with a person in the story.

Hold the Bible in your hand or lap as you tell a Bible story.

State clearly that the stories in the Bible are true — they really happened.

Introduce the story by talking about familiar experiences of the children which are similar to events in the story.

Show visuals of Bible story people and places to increase and clarify children's understanding. Pictures help children see the story as having really happened. A model of a Bible-time house or well, for example, helps make those items clear in their minds when a story involves such items.

A significant part of presenting a Bible story to young children is talking about the story they've just heard. Simple questions such as, "What did the shepherds care for out on the hillside?" and "What did the wise men see shining brightly in the nighttime sky?" help children recall story facts. (The wise teacher does not let a child flounder in answering, but gives a clue or shows an appropriate picture.) Kindergartners also enjoy responding to questions which require reasoning. "Why did Jesus want to visit at Zacchaeus' house?" challenges young listeners. Open-ended questions such as, "Which part of the story did you like best?" or "What do you think happened next?" also find a ready response. Since there is no right or wrong answer, the child feels safe in answering.

(Continued.)

EARLY CHILDHOOD

Making the Connection with Today's Kids

(Continued.)

Bible Learning Activities

Much of what we want to help a child learn from the Bible has to do with abstract concepts such as love, kindness, self-worth, respect and concern for others. These abstract ideas which a child cannot touch or see are more difficult to understand than specific items—such as an apple, for instance. When we use only words, we expect children to imagine in their mind's eye a picture (based on previous experience) of what we mean. Since a young child's experience is limited, his or her interpretation of our words could be very different than what we intended. How can we help children learn biblical truths that involve abstract concepts—things which cannot be seen?

Know that firsthand experiences are the core of children's learning. A young child learns by doing. And doing to that child means playing. Play is his or her work and education. Bible Learning Activities—play with a purpose—are designed to give children firsthand experiences in learning the meaning of abstract words such as love, kindness and thankfulness. But to help children understand what these words mean in their own experience and in relation to God's Word, a teacher must be nearby to guide, identify and commend certain actions. For example, when a child willingly shares with another, the teacher first describes this action. "Seth did not have enough dough. Ashley gave Seth some of her dough." Then the teacher applies the idea to the action. "That's sharing. I'm glad Ashley knows how to share! Our Bible says, *Share with others.*" Be ready for times to connect a child's actions with God's Word.

Bible Memorization

Because young children are here-and-now people, they need to sense an immediate relation between their situation and what God's Word says. For example, when Cory hears *help each other* spoken as she is helping a younger child complete a puzzle, Cory can relate those words to her actions. "Cory, helping Shannon finish her puzzle is doing just what our Bible says, *Help each other,*" her teacher comments.

During the Together Time part of the session, Cory hears *help each other* read from the Bible. She joins other children and teachers in singing these Bible words several times. As Cory completes her Activity Page illustrating *help each other*, she hears her teacher read those words printed on the picture. Again and again through conversation, songs and explanation, teachers help lay a groundwork of familiarity coupled with understanding. Memorization of Bible verses happens naturally as they are repeatedly used to accompany the child's activities. While being able to say the words is valuable, for a young child, **understanding** is the primary aim.

God's long-range goal for every child and adult is that he or she may "reach unity in the faith and in the knowledge of the Son of God and become mature, attaining to the whole measure of the fullness of Christ" (Ephesians 4:13, *NIV*). The earliest beginning of this great process occurs as loving Christian adults work patiently in a wide variety of learning experiences, introducing God's Word in ways that connect with the child's level of development and understanding.

Few things more effectively communicate the significance of God's Word to a child than the attitude and actions of the adults around them. When a child senses a teacher's enthusiasm for God's Word and interest in telling a Bible story, he or she will also come to value and respect God's Word.

Through the entire session let your children hear God's Word connected to their actions. Allow them to live it. They will sense that Bible truth is not separated from life, but a real part of it.

Bible Study Tool for Teachers

EARLY CHILDHOOD/CHILDREN

To be a teacher of the Word, one must also be a student of the Word. Often teachers focus their lesson preparation mostly on their presentation of activities and the Bible story, overlooking the rich benefits to be gained from meditating on the meaning and purpose of a passage to be taught. Use this simple outline as a tool in making personal Bible study rewarding for yourself as well as your students.

Lesson Scripture passage:

1. What does this passage say? What are the key words, phrases, ideas, events, etc.?

2. What does it mean? How are the key words, phrases, ideas and events to be properly interpreted?

3. How does it apply to contemporary life?

For people in general:

For me personally:

For children in my class:

Sharing Your Classroom Space

✦ At the beginning of the school year, meet with the teacher(s) with whom you share a classroom. Talk about the needs of each program and make specific plans about how to help each other. Come to an agreement on the best arrangement of furniture and equipment. Plan to remove any furnishings or supplies not in use by either program. If possible, try to have the same age groups using the same rooms. Plan a system of ongoing communication.

✦ If the classroom will be used by children of the same age, plan to share equipment and as many supplies as possible. Make decisions ahead of time about the use of the shared equipment. What can be placed on the walls or bulletin boards? When are the wastebaskets to be emptied? How much cleanup must be done by teachers and what can the custodial staff be expected to do? What should be done with materials accidentally left in the classroom?

✦ If you have a problem with materials disappearing, locked storage space should be requested for your classroom. If locked storage space in the classroom is limited, purchase some sturdy cardboard file boxes. Label each one with the type of material it contains. Then, either store the cartons in another room in the building where they will not be disturbed, or arrange for teachers to bring them to each session.

✦ Consider using portable storage carts. Carts can be purchased or built. When the materials on the cart are not being used, the cart may be kept in a central supply room.

✦ If sharing bulletin boards is a problem, either assign each board for use by a different class, or build reversible bulletin boards. Another option is to make a portable bulletin board (fiberboard covered with fabric) which can be hung over a permanent board.

✦ Open shelves on wheels can be turned to the wall when not in use.

✦ If a custodian's help is available, give him or her clear diagrams for the room arrangements for each class.

Communication Handicaps

Learning to talk doesn't always "just happen." A teacher is likely to have at least one child who experiences difficulty making correct speech sounds, putting words together to make meaningful sentences, or properly making sense of what is said to him or her. Some children may experience all three of these difficulties.

Following are some general guidelines for helping the child with communication handicaps.

Speech

Some children, especially at younger ages, have difficulty correctly producing some of the later-developing speech sounds, such as *r* and *s*. Words such as "rabbit" and "sun" become "wabbit" and "thun." These speech errors are fairly typical and it is not difficult to understand the intended meaning.

But what about the child who has difficulty correctly producing *many* sounds? Often, people feel uncomfortable asking a child to repeat something that wasn't clear enough to be understood. A common response is to pretend to understand. But this is frustrating to the child, especially when the child asks a specific question and receives a vague statement in reply.

By far the better thing to do is to say to the child, "Eric, I didn't understand what you said. Please say it again." If Eric's second attempt is not distinct enough to be understood, encourage him to show you what he means. Ask him to act out what he wants or to point to the thing about which he is speaking. Or, ask if he needs or wants something.

If you are still unable to learn what the child has said, be honest about it. "Eric, I'm still not sure what you are telling me. When your mom comes, maybe she can help me understand." Let Eric know that, even though you were unable to understand, you feel that what he said is important enough to try again later.

Language

"Language" refers to the way words are strung together to make meaningful statements. A child whose language level seems "younger" than that of other children in the class may be experiencing a delay in the development of language. There are several methods that are very helpful to a child in a classroom environment. These methods will not instantly produce age-level language skills, but over a period of time, they usually produce positive results.

One method is called *expansion.* The teacher repeats what the child says, but "cleans up" the grammar. For instance, the child says, "Her taked my block." The teacher "expands" the child's grammatical form: "She took your block? Let's find another block for her." This method is more effective than calling attention to the incorrect grammar (as in "We don't say 'taked.' We say 'took.'").

Another way to help the child is the use of *parallel talk.* As Lindy is playing, describe what she is doing. "Lindy, you are building a house. You are building a house with the blocks. I see you are driving the car to the house." When Lindy hears the words to describe what she is doing, language learning takes place.

(Continued.)

Communication Handicaps

(Continued.)

Understanding

Some children may not have developed adequate language processing skills. They hear the words, but are not yet able to understand all of what is being said. It is important to remember that children are still learning the intricacies of our language. Many children who appear to be disobeying may not have correctly understood what was said. When working on an activity, go to the individual child and speak directly to him or her. Give only one instruction at a time. For example, rather than saying, "Put the pencil where it belongs," name each individual step necessary for completing the task. "Chris, pick up the pencil." (Wait for correct response.) "Now put the pencil in the can." Sometimes it is helpful to demonstrate what you mean.

Children are special people. They want, just as adults do, to understand and be understood. As you pray for your class each week, ask God to help you find ways to encourage that child who often is frustrated in trying to communicate.

Also, ask the child's parents what ways they have found to be helpful in communicating with their child. If they express concerns about their child's speech, language or understanding, encourage them to contact a speech and language specialist in the area (at a public school, private practice, hospital, or community speech, language and hearing center).

Hearing Impairments

EARLY CHILDHOOD/CHILDREN

Children with hearing impairments are as diverse as children who hear normally. It is essential to realize that a hearing loss is *not* a loss of intellectual ability. In most cases, you should be able to expect what is socially and educationally appropriate for a child of that age. Do not underestimate a child with a hearing impairment!

Following are some suggestions and information to guide you in teaching a child with a hearing impairment.

Communication Skills

May include oral (speech, lip reading, and listening with hearing aids), manual (sign language and finger spelling), or total communication (all of the above). Talk with parents about their child's present oral or manual vocabulary to help you to determine an appropriate language level to use when teaching the child. Meet with the parents at the beginning of each unit or quarter to inform them of the concepts you will be teaching and the vocabulary words you will be using. Encourage the parents to work with their child during the week with any new vocabulary words that will be used in next week's lesson.

Sign Language

If signing is the child's main means of communication, have the parents teach you some basic signs: The child's name sign, key words for each quarter (e.g., Jesus, dead, alive), simple directions (e.g., "Sit down," "Come," "Stop"), and some friendly signs (e.g., "Thank you," "I'm glad to see you," "You are helping"). Encourage the other children to learn some of the signs. You may want to borrow a sign language book from the parents.

Hearing Aids

Ask the parents to show you how their child's hearing aid works. You will need to know if it is adjusted to the appropriate volume setting. The young child often "adjusts" his or her aid by turning the volume too high, too low or, yes—even off.

The presence of a hearing aid in a child's ear will arouse curiosity in other children. You may tell them that a hearing aid helps people to hear like glasses help people to see. (This is not a totally accurate comparison, but it will enable young children to understand the purpose of a hearing aid.)

Since a hearing aid amplifies *all* sounds, keep in mind that the hearing impaired child will find it difficult to understand a person talking in a noisy environment.

Speech

Speak naturally, at a moderate rate, emphasizing the key word. Speaking loudly will distort rather than clarify your speech. Exaggerating your lip movement or facial expression makes your speech harder to understand.

✦ Your lips must be seen. Wait for a look from the child before you begin to speak. If you are showing something to the children during an activity, show the object first. Then wait for a look from the child before you begin talking about the object.

(Continued.)

◆ Keep gestures to a minimum as you speak unless they are specific signs which the child understands.

◆ Feel free to talk to the hearing impaired child about his or her speech. There may be times when the child will need to be told to speak softer or louder.

◆ If you do not understand something the child says, do not pretend that you do! Instead, ask the child to repeat what he or she said. If possible, ask the child to show or act out what he or she said. If you still do not comprehend, tell the child, "I don't know what you said. We will ask your mom and dad to help us later." (You may want to have the other children help you. Children often understand other children more clearly than an adult does.)

Language

Use as high a level of language as you think the child will comprehend. Don't talk "baby talk" or talk "down" to the child.

◆ Talk in complete phrases or short sentences.

◆ After you have given specific directions for an activity, ask the hearing impaired child to repeat what he or she understands you to have said. (e.g., "Devon, please tell me what I said.") Allow the child to answer without giving him or her any negative response for answering incorrectly. The child's understanding is based on partially heard and therefore partially understood information.

◆ Rephrasing and restating information is especially helpful for the hearing impaired.

◆ Always accept what the hearing impaired child says if the idea is correct regardless of his or her grammar. "Model" the appropriate grammar for the child. For example, if the child says, "Me love Jesus," say "Good, I love Jesus, too."

Activities

Do not underestimate the hearing impaired child's ability to participate in all areas of the session. During an activity song in which children suggest actions for the song, encourage the hearing impaired child to share his or her idea by pantomiming the movement. Hearing impaired children, including the profoundly deaf, enjoy music.

Love

All children respond positively to love. It is one of the best ways God has given us to communicate with each other. Express this love in words ("God loves you. And I love you, too."), with facial expressions (warm smiles) and through touch (a squeeze of the hand, a hug, a pat on the shoulder).

Physical Handicaps

You may have an opportunity sometime to teach a child who has a physical handicap. The handicap may be relatively mild or it may be severe. In either case, it is very important to talk with the parents of the child as soon as the child joins your class.

When you talk with the parents, ask how they would prefer you explain their child's handicap to the other children in the class. A detailed explanation is not necessary, but it should be honest and sufficient to satisfy the other children's curiosity. It should also be presented in a manner that makes the other children feel more comfortable with the handicapped child. For example, you might say, "Brian's legs don't work the same as ours, so he needs a wheelchair to be able to move around. Sometimes, Brian might like you to push his wheelchair, if you're very careful."

Activities

Briefly explain to the parents the type of learning activities that take place in your classroom. Then invite parents to describe their child's abilities in relation to the learning activities. For example, if the child's arm or hand muscles are only slightly impaired, an art activity that doesn't require a great deal of precision may be entirely appropriate. The parents should be able to give you this kind of information. It is very important to focus on the child's *abilities*—the things he or she *is* capable of doing.

Abilities

You may want to invite the child's parents to attend a class session. This will enable them to evaluate the activities in order to advise you about their child's ability to participate. It will also give you an opportunity to observe the parents and their method of handling the child's handicap. For example, the child may be able to hold a crayon or a pencil if his or her fingers are moved to the correct position. The parents will be glad to demonstrate the best methods of working with their child.

If the child's handicap is such that it is not possible for him or her to work on certain parts of a learning activity, complete those parts ahead of time and focus on something the child can do to complete the activity. The handicapped child that is unable to work on an activity can tell you or another child what needs to be done to complete the activity. Be sure to include the child in conversation to help him or her feel a part of the activity.

If the child is severely handicapped, you may need to invite an additional adult to join your teaching staff. There are often people who feel uncomfortable with a large group of children, but would welcome an opportunity to minister to the needs of one child.

Love

The most important aspect of time spent together is not the actual participation in the activities; it is the experience of God's love. Pray that God will guide you in choosing and recognizing creative and meaningful ways to involve the child as much as possible in each class session. Also pray for sensitivity to the child's special needs, as well as for the family's needs.

Visual Handicaps

EARLY CHILDHOOD/CHILDREN

If you have a partially-sighted or blind child in your classroom, the following guidelines are designed to help both you and the child feel more comfortable.

Acceptance

As far as possible, treat the child as you would any other child. Include him or her in all activities. Apply the same classroom rules to the visually-handicapped child that apply to the other children. Be a good role model by showing warm acceptance of the child. Let the child do as much as he or she can.

◆ Encourage the child to use his or her vision. Sight is not conserved by not using it.

◆ When the other children ask questions about the child's visual handicap, encourage the child to answer these questions. Often a child's simple, straightforward answer satisfies the curiosity of other children. If the child is shy or reluctant to answer, say, "Everyone sees differently. Joshua doesn't see the way we do." If questions persist, ask the parents for suggestions.

◆ Talk to him or her as you would to any other child. There's no need to avoid the use of words such as "see" and "look." Many visually-handicapped children see objects by looking at them very closely. Others with less sight use the words "see" and "look" when they touch an object to get a feel for how it "looks."

Communication

Speak in a normal voice. When speaking specifically to the visually-handicapped child, use his or her name. And tell the child who you are. "Hi, Michael. I'm Miss Robbins."

◆ To best help the visually-handicapped child become familiar with the classroom, encourage the child to explore the classroom with you. Never grab the child. Rather, offer your hand by gently tapping his or her hand. As you walk with the child around the room, encourage him or her to touch furniture and materials to see where the items are kept. Always keep furniture and supplies in the same place from week to week. Describe what activities take place in each area of the room.

Activities

Seat the child near visual aids, but still within the group of children. Allow the child to get as close to materials as he or she desires (or, if appropriate, to bring materials close to him- or herself). Allow the child to explore materials by touch.

During the activities, instructions are often visual in nature, such as, "Fold your paper like I'm folding mine." In this case, bring your hands within the visually-handicapped child's range. Or, let the child touch your paper to learn how you are folding it. Also, make use of verbal cues: describe pictures, explain activities, talk about actions you see in the classroom, etc.

Love

For a visually-handicapped child, the sense of touch is deeply important. Express your love and caring for the child with gentle touches and hugs.

The Leader's Role— Building the Team

EARLY CHILDHOOD/CHILDREN

The following guidelines summarize the basic tasks involved in supporting and building successful teaching teams.

Basic Function

✦ Prayerfully build relationships with both teachers and children in order to ensure effective Bible learning.

NOTE: In a department with just two teachers, the leader responsibilities may be informally shared. When three or more people are on the team, one person should be designated as Lead Teacher or Department Leader.

Class Responsibilities

✦ Coordinate teacher tasks, including use of supplies and room setup.

✦ Greet children as they arrive and guide them to an activity (Early Childhood) or class group (Children).

✦ Assist teachers as needed (e.g., discipline, activity completion, etc.), maintaining the time schedule for the session.

✦ Observe, affirm and evaluate teachers at work in order to note strengths to encourage and areas where improvement is possible.

✦ Lead the large group learning time, involving other teachers as appropriate.

NOTE: In smaller departments, the leader may guide an activity or class group. In larger departments (18 or more children), it is best if the leader is free to move among the activities being led by teachers.

Team Responsibilities

✦ Pray regularly for others on your teaching team.

✦ Work with your church leadership to identify and enlist qualified people to join your teaching team.

✦ Consistently affirm teachers for their efforts and faithfulness.

✦ Seek to improve the effectiveness of your teaching team by leading regular training/planning meetings which provide opportunities for spiritual growth and development of teaching skills.

✦ Encourage teachers in their out-of-class efforts to build relationships with children and their families, focusing on followup strategies for visitors and absentees.

✦ Channel communications between church leadership and your teaching team.

The Teacher's Role— Nurturing Children

EARLY CHILDHOOD/CHILDREN

The following guidelines summarize the basic tasks involved in nurturing the spiritual growth of children.

Basic Function

Prayerfully build relationships with children in order to guide and involve them in life-changing Bible learning.

Class Responsibilities

✦ Arrange materials and room to create an effective learning environment.

✦ Greet each child upon arrival and engage him or her in conversation and meaningful activity.

✦ Model the love of Christ and the power of God's Word and the Holy Spirit in ways that are appropriate to the age level of the class.

✦ Show love and concern for children by getting to know them, accepting them as they are, actively listening to them and sharing their concerns, needs, and joys.

✦ Affirm and support children for specific evidences of growth and learning.

✦ Guide Bible learning by:
—being well-prepared to use Bible stories, verses/passages, questions and comments appropriate to the age level in order to accomplish the lesson aims;
—connecting Bible content to needs and interests;
—selecting challenging Bible learning methods;
—encouraging children to be honest in expressing their ideas and feelings;
—helping children explore and apply Bible truths to achieve understanding and lead to changes in attitude and behavior.

✦ Participate with children in learning activities and in large-group times.

✦ Observe and evaluate children's progress.

Out-of-Class Responsibilities

✦ Pray regularly for each child.

✦ Cultivate the friendship and interests of children and their families, seeking to win unchurched families to Christ and the church.

✦ Show love and concern by following up on visitors and absentees.

Team Responsibilities

✦ Pray regularly for others on your teaching team.

✦ Seek to identify and recommend people to join your teaching team.

✦ Improve the effectiveness of your teaching team by participating regularly in training/planning meetings.

NOTE: Just as Jesus sent His followers out in pairs, and to meet the variety of needs and interests in any group of children, all teachers should serve on teams so at least two teachers are in the room at all times. This staffing also ensures a responsible person is available in case an emergency arises, and provides protection for the teachers should any question ever be raised about how children are being treated.

Reaching Out to God's Family Around the World

"God, please bless the missionaries!" some Sunday School children dutifully pray. However, they may have little or no idea of who these "missionaries" are, nor of what it is they are asking God to do for them.

Teachers, this general prayer is all you can expect them to pray unless you give the children in your class a specific need to pray about, or a specific project to which they can give money or time. Below are several specific projects your department can consider for a focus on world missions. These projects require preparation so begin your planning a month or two in advance. Focus on the unique ministries of your church or denomination as you prepare.

Get addresses of missionaries to whom the children can write. Choose missionaries in various occupations. Select one field or various locations. It is especially effective if one or more missionaries have children close in age to the children in your class.

Write to these missionaries. Say, for example, "In four or five weeks children in our Sunday School will be studying missions. In order to make our study more meaningful we would appreciate your letting us know (1) information about the country in which you live; (2) your job; (3) specific things we can pray about; and (4) a project or small gift of money we can share with you." Ask the missionary what is the best way to reimburse him or her for expenses.

Research prayer needs of missionaries. It is important to find out specific prayer requests. Pool information from staff and church members. List needs each missionary may have—money, supplies, friends, schools for children. Does he or she need prayer for learning a new language? Prayer for more believers? Prayer that believers grow in their faith? Research these needs and children can begin to pray specifically and thank God for specific answers!

Plan a project to involve the children in giving their time, money or possessions to help a missionary. Contact your church missions committee or denominational office for information. Or, the idea for your project may come directly from your correspondence with the missionaries. You may choose to make puppets; collect greeting cards, food, clothing, toys, books; cut out magazine pictures. Your students will be pleased to have such a special role.

Make a tabletop display for your project (see sketch). Let the children suggest what they can do without, such as ice cream, candy, toys, part of their allowance. Suggest several household chores children may offer to do for money to contribute. Use a glass jar to collect the visible results. After you have collected addresses of missionaries, written to let them know what to expect, compiled a list of specific prayer requests and planned a project, you may wish to choose from the following ideas to enhance the children's understanding and involvement in missions.

1. Schedule a **visitor** to tell a true mission story. Your guest may be a missionary or one who has visited a mission field. Use high school or college students who have been on short-term mission assignments. Before the guest arrives, have the children write or dictate questions to ask. Later they can make a report as a group about what they have learned.

(Continued.)

What Can We Give Up to Help the People in India?

ICE CREAM | CANDY | TOYS | PART OF ALLOWANCE

EARLY CHILDHOOD/CHILDREN

Reaching Out to God's Family Around the World

(Continued.)

2. Begin a **cassette tape exchange.** Make a cassette tape to mail to your missionaries. Include songs and Bible verses from the group, news about your Sunday School activities, and questions the children want to ask.

Let the children do the asking. "Hello! My name is Adam. I would like to know if . . . ?" The missionary will be able to answer Adam (and the group) specifically.

Also, record the children praying for missions. The prayers of the children will encourage the missionaries.

Leave room at the end of the tape for missionaries to reply with songs, news and answers to questions. Send a self-addressed, stamped cassette mailer for return of the tape.

3. Make a **display** for others in your church to see. Supply the missionaries with an international money order to purchase curios you can display. (Or, items may be purchased from an imported goods store.) Have the children plan the display. The ideas behind the display will remain with them longer if they have had a part in the planning.

4. Make a chart listing the **birthdays of missionaries and their children.** Make cards for upcoming birthdays and/or holidays.

5. Listen to a **recording in the language of a missionary's country and learn a song** in that language.

6. Have a **picture exchange.** Duplicate missionary pictures so each child in your class can use them to make prayer reminders. Send pictures of the children in your class to the missionaries so they can also have prayer reminders for you.

7. View a missions film or video.

8. Prepare a missions listening post. Record a missionary story on cassette tape for children to hear with earphones.

9. Set up a missions book corner in your classroom. Purchase or borrow one or more children's books about the lives of famous missionaries.

A Child's Healthy Self-Esteem

EARLY CHILDHOOD/CHILDREN

Ingredients:

1. Unconditional love. Love must not depend on perfect behavior or appearance. Each child is to be loved for who he or she is—a unique, special creation of God's. If we focus on outer qualities, we will miss the attributes that make each child unique. Unconditional love does not mean approving negative things a child does. It simply recognizes the vast difference between *doing* an undesirable thing and *being* an undesirable person.

Mrs. Adams found Jessamyn rummaging through a desk drawer. "Jessamyn! Get out of there!" she yelled. "You're a naughty girl." Mrs. Adams was telling Jessamyn *what she was* instead of dealing with *what Jessamyn did*. A better approach would be to say, "Jessamyn, the drawer needs to be kept closed."

2. Appreciation for the child. We all want to know we are appreciated by our families and our church. Children want to know this, too. A child needs to know, "My teachers are glad to have me here." By showing appreciation for a child, we communicate that the child is loved by God and people.

3. Sense of accomplishment. It is satisfying to a child when he or she completes a task. Finishing a job says that the child is a capable person. Learning to ride a bike, read a book, button a shirt or work a puzzle are only a few of the tasks children seek to learn.

Do Not Add the Following:

1. Criticism. When we focus on a child's shortcomings, it is a blow to a child's self-esteem. The child equates criticism of work with criticism of person, and therefore feels rebellion, humiliation or rejection. Remarks such as "You're too little," "You did it wrong again," "Here, let me do that," have a negative impact on a child. Instead, say, "You've made a good start" or, "If you decide you need help with that, let me know."

2. Insensitivity which causes embarrassment can also cause damage. Sarcasm or ridicule, especially in front of others, has a demeaning effect on children. We can also hurt a child by talking about him or her as if that child were not there. And punishing a child in public is particularly embarrassing to the child. Discipline should be a private matter, not only to help a child retain dignity but to avoid having others magnify the problem. One teacher realized he had acted unwisely in reprimanding Anthony where other children could hear. Over a period of weeks he heard children talking to Anthony in the same reprimanding manner. Anthony, who desperately needed approval, was now being rejected by others. The teacher made a point to publicly praise and encourage Anthony for his behavior.

3. A **lack of respect** is shown in what we say and don't say to children. "Thank you," "please," "excuse me," and especially, "I'm sorry" are phrases children may not often hear from us. Children need to receive the same common courtesies we do. (The child will imitate our example of courtesy or discourtesy.)

Sometimes we incorrectly assume we have the right to interrupt children for any reason, insisting that children stop whatever they are doing when we speak. We need to ask ourselves, "Would I say this to another adult? Would I treat another adult this way?" We need to consider what we model when we abruptly interrupt a child's activity or conversation. We may actually delay the child learning to show respect for others.

4. Lack of encouragement. Children need verbal encouragement, even for common tasks. We may not think it is important to give praise for things a child "is supposed to do." However, most children need encouragement and recognition to help them *want* to do what they are *supposed* to do. "Good try" and "I like it when you put away the pencils" are simple statements that encourage a child. Even simply acknowledging a child's act with an "I see..." statement will encourage him or her. "I see you put the pencils away."

(Continued.)

SELF-ESTEEM

A Child's Healthy Self-Esteem

(Continued.)

5. Comparisons. Statements such as "You're just like your sister" or "Why can't you be like Megan?" are *devastating*. It is important to remember that God designs originals—no copies. Each of His creations is unique. Each child needs to be welcomed for who he or she is and helped to achieve his or her own unique potential. To the Master Artist, each work is a masterpiece. Reflect His love; do not compare children.

6. Overprotectiveness. Baby birds would die in their nests unless the parent bird encouraged them to fly. Parents and teachers often want to shield children from dangerous and unpleasant experiences. However, when we insist on doing things the child should be learning to do, or restricting a child's exploration for fear of failure, we damage the child's ability to develop. Provide a safe environment in which children can freely learn and investigate, and let them explore.

7. Punishment rather than discipline. These words are significantly different. Punishment is retaliation for wrongdoing. Discipline is an instructional process which includes encouragement as well as correction. Punishment focuses on getting even. Discipline carries the message of "I love you and want to help you do the right thing." Punishment arouses guilt, fear, anger, and sometimes hatred. Discipline inspires love, concern and a desire to improve.

Ryan was often disruptive. His teacher had tried reprimands, isolation and removal of privileges. Miss Wong noticed a growing resentment in Ryan. She took Ryan aside. "Ryan, it seems hard for you to do what the teachers want. You must be unhappy about this." For the first time a teacher was seeking to understand Ryan, not just control him. "I'd like to help you learn to do some things that are hard for you. We can work together if you want." Ryan smiled at Miss Wong. The process of discipline had begun.

Meeting the Needs of Students Checklist

EARLY CHILDHOOD/CHILDREN

Use this checklist as a tool to evaluate the ways in which you meet the needs of the students in your class. Check the box which most correctly answers each of the questions below.

	ALWAYS	OFTEN	SOMETIMES	SELDOM	NEVER

Physical

DO YOU...

	ALWAYS	OFTEN	SOMETIMES	SELDOM	NEVER
◆ provide adequate lighting for reading?	☐	☐	☐	☐	☐
◆ keep the room temperature and air circulation comfortable?	☐	☐	☐	☐	☐
◆ arrange furnishings to encourage participation?	☐	☐	☐	☐	☐
◆ plan a variety of styles of learning activities during the quarter?	☐	☐	☐	☐	☐

Emotional/Mental

DO YOU...

	ALWAYS	OFTEN	SOMETIMES	SELDOM	NEVER
◆ show sensitivity to your children's problems and feelings?	☐	☐	☐	☐	☐
◆ share personal feelings and experiences from your Christian life?	☐	☐	☐	☐	☐
◆ encourage your children to work together?	☐	☐	☐	☐	☐
◆ provide the security of a few rules that are consistently enforced?	☐	☐	☐	☐	☐

Social

DO YOU...

	ALWAYS	OFTEN	SOMETIMES	SELDOM	NEVER
◆ avoid using "put-downs" when opinions or ideas are different from yours?	☐	☐	☐	☐	☐
◆ see your class as individuals rather than as a group?	☐	☐	☐	☐	☐
◆ listen to your children?	☐	☐	☐	☐	☐
◆ affirm your children for sharing and cooperating in class?	☐	☐	☐	☐	☐
◆ provide creative ways for children to express ideas and use abilities, interests?	☐	☐	☐	☐	☐
◆ plan ways to involve each child?	☐	☐	☐	☐	☐
◆ have an awareness of the vocabulary level of your children?	☐	☐	☐	☐	☐

Spiritual

DO YOU...

	ALWAYS	OFTEN	SOMETIMES	SELDOM	NEVER
◆ help your children discover Bible truths for themselves?	☐	☐	☐	☐	☐
◆ help your children identify with Bible characters as real people?	☐	☐	☐	☐	☐
◆ actively seek to discover each child's spiritual condition and attitudes?	☐	☐	☐	☐	☐
◆ express enthusiasm about being a Christian?	☐	☐	☐	☐	☐

How Art Helps Children Learn Bible Truths

CHILDREN

Bible Learning Activities involving creative art experiences provide an enjoyable and effective way for children to express what they have learned and to plan ways to put that learning into action. As you use art activities, remember that the learning *process* is more important than the end *product*. As you select and use art experiences, focus the child's attention on the Bible truth concerned, not on the result or quality of the work.

For example:

◆ as a child works to portray an incident in the Bible story, the teacher should ask questions to stimulate the child to rethink the narrative: "What happened just before the scene you are making?"

"Which person in this scene is a good example to follow? Why?"

The teacher should also ask questions to help the child focus on the main truth illustrated in the story:

"What did you learn about friendship from the story of David?"

"What could you do this week that would show kindness as David did?"

◆ as a child draws or paints or models a contemporary scene, the teacher should connect this familiar experience to the Bible story or Bible verse:

"What are you doing in this picture that is the same as what Ruth did in our story?"

"How would it help the person in your picture if he/she remembered our Bible verse?"

Benefits of Art Activities

Lesson-related art activities can help a child:

◆ show in a concrete way an abstract concept such as loving, forgiving, worshiping, serving;

◆ think in terms of specific actions (clean my room, take out the trash) as he/she applies a Bible verse such as "Children, obey your parents" (Ephesians 6:1, *NIV*);

◆ discover/show new learnings (for example, illustrating in proper sequence the events of a Bible story);

◆ put into practice Bible truths (for example, showing love to others by making tray favors for residents in a convalescent home);

◆ express thoughts that may be difficult to put into words (such as illustrating a scene from a Bible story).

Tips for Leading Art Activities

◆ Before children begin using the art materials, ask each one to tell his or her idea for a picture, scene, etc.

◆ If an activity requires use of a material which is new to you, or if the activity involves several steps, make a sample before class.

◆ Materials for art activities are limited only by your imagination. Enlist the help of interested parents and church members in collecting and labeling items. List the articles you need in your church newsletter or bulletin.

◆ Store materials and equipment in an organized way where children can see and reach them. Label containers and shelves so children can easily return items to their proper places.

◆ You may want to cover tables with plastic tablecloths or newspapers in order to make cleanup easy.

◆ Keep paper towels or sponges handy so that cleanup will be easy when a spill occurs.

Kids Learn Best Through Activity

CHILDREN

Bible Learning Activities are creative activities designed to reinforce Bible truths. These hands-on activities may involve art, music, writing, drama or other skills. But each activity will help children apply Bible truths to their lives. What qualifies an activity for use at Sunday School? How can we be certain that the activity will result in Bible learning? When does an activity become a Bible Learning Activity?

The activity must fit these criteria in order to be used as a Bible Learning Activity:

Question 1: Does it teach, review or reinforce a Bible truth?

Question 2: Does the Bible Learning Activity encourage use of the Bible and biblically oriented tools such as dictionaries, encyclopedias, maps, etc.?

Question 3: Will the activity give the child an opportunity to relate the Bible truth to his or her everyday experiences? As the relevance of Bible truth becomes apparent to the child, the teacher then needs to help the child plan for specific ways to make the Bible truth a part of his or her day-to-day actions. The teacher also needs to follow up, in order to be aware of what happened when the child attempted to put the Bible truth into practice. This kind of follow-up provides a basis for teacher-child evaluation. It also permits the teacher to be supportive and encouraging as the child moves toward changing his or her behavior, a true test of learning.

Be Specific, Yet Flexible

Each Bible Learning Activity must be specific enough to permit the child to feel assured (as the activity develops) that the activity has purpose. However, it must be flexible enough to take into account the ability and skill level of each child.

For example, as a teacher prepares for a Bible Learning Activity in which puppets will be used to dramatize a Bible story, that teacher will make sure the activity includes both academic and nonacademic-oriented tasks (writing and reading the scripts as well as making and using the puppets). A teacher also will offer children opportunities to participate in planning. Often a child's ideas help make the activity more effective than if only the plans of the teacher were used. Then the teacher is not only a learning guide, but also a learner along with the children.

How to Guide Activities

Five main steps are needed for learning to take place in an activity:

1. Introduce the purpose of each activity.

When an activity is first presented to children, it is important to explain *why* the children will be doing it, and not simply *what* they will do. For example, children may choose an art activity because they like to draw cartoons. Help them see beyond the procedures to the purpose: e.g., "to help us learn ways to trust God in hard times."

2. Involve children in research.

While research may occasionally be an activity all by itself, all other types of activities need to begin with having the children review or gather some specific Bible information. The method for this research must be compatible with children's ability and interests. For example, a first grader may simply read Bible words the teacher has lettered on a chalkboard, while a fifth grader will locate and read the verses in the Bible. The older child might use a Bible dictionary to look up any word he does not understand, while the younger child may look at pictures or listen to a taped explanation.

(Continued.)

3. Guide the conversation to emphasize the purpose of the activity.

As children work on an activity, the teacher uses informal conversation to guide a child's thoughts, feelings and words toward the lesson focus. For example, as a role-play activity begins to lose focus, the teacher might ask one of the players, "What would Michael say to his mom to show he really wanted to do what was right, like our Bible verse says?" Quickly the participants will refocus on the point of the activity.

By being alert to relate the child's experience to what God's Word says, a teacher helps that child understand Bible truth.

4. Lead children to identify what they are learning by doing the activity.

As children near the completion of an activity, the teacher should ask them to put into words what they have learned about the main truth of the lesson: "What have you learned about forgiveness today? What information did you discover about Paul and his missionary journeys today?" When children find such a question difficult to answer, the teacher knows that more learning is needed.

5. Lead children in sharing with others what they learned.

One of the most important steps in the learning process is sharing with someone else what was learned. Children need to be encouraged to do this on a regular basis:

◆ Asking the child to think of what to tell someone else about an activity is a helpful way to lead the child to think of the point of a lesson. "If you were to tell a friend about this activity, how would you explain what you've learned about Jesus and the children?"

◆ Give children an opportunity to share their Bible Learning Activities with those in other groups. This sharing of activities can be done in a variety of ways. Children can show what they did while the teacher explains it. The teacher can ask questions to lead children in explaining what they learned. A few children can speak on behalf of the rest of their group. Each group member can offer one or two sentences to tell the most important (or interesting) thing they learned.

◆ Occasionally you may. arrange for a group of children to display and explain their activity to children in a different age level.

Hide God's Word in Your Heart

Discovering truths from God's Word can be an exciting and rewarding experience for all children in your class. Some children may memorize easily as they enjoy these activities. Other children may have difficulty recalling all the words, but can still clearly understand the meaning of the passage. Be sensitive to the learning level and learning style of each child. Each is an individual and has a different capacity to memorize and recall. Here are some ideas for helping children understand and memorize God's Word.

✦ Use the Bible Memory Verse as often as possible in your natural conversation and discussion during each activity.

✦ Ask questions to check a child's understanding of a specific Bible passage. For example, "How would you say this Bible verse in your own words? What are ways these verses can help you at school? In the neighborhood?

With your family? What do you think is the most important word in this Bible verse? Why?"

✦ Occasionally share situations in which knowing God's Word has helped you. Repeat a specific Bible verse that has special significance for you.

✦ Use the variety of ways Bible verses are presented and discussed in your curriculum.

> **Use the Bible Memory Verse in your natural conversation and discussion.**

Games, worksheets, Bible Learning Activities and songs encourage children's understanding and practical application of each Bible Memory Verse. As you lead children in activities, encourage them to memorize God's Word and give honest encouragement for each child's efforts.

✦ Rather than individual memorization contests which often discourage children for whom memorization is difficult, challenge your students to work together to achieve a class goal. For example, explain that when 30 verses have been memorized by the class, a special treat will be provided. Make the first goal one that should be achievable within a month. The second goal can require additional work. Points toward the class goal may be achieved through Bible memorization, attendance, bringing a Bible to class, etc. Provide a visual reminder of the goal and a means for children to record their progress. For example, children may add construction paper loops to a chain, color in a square on a chart, add a marble to a jar or attach a sticker to a chart to show each point earned.

Above all, remember that your own attitude toward God's Word and your memorization of Bible verses will have the greatest affect on children as you encourage them to "hide God's Word in their hearts." (See Psalm 119:11.)

What to Expect from Kids in Grades 1 and 2

CHILDREN

Physical

Children need opportunities for movement during every class session. Small muscle coordination is still developing and improving. Girls are ahead of boys at this stage of development. **Teaching Tips**: Use activities that involve cutting and simple writing skills; give alternatives for children who do not write well (e.g., drawing); give children opportunities to change positions and to move about the room; vary the activities.

Emotional

Children are experiencing new and frequently intense feelings as they grow in independence. Sometimes the child finds it hard to control his or her behavior. There is still a deep need for approval from adults and a growing need for approval by peers. **Teaching Tips:** Seek opportunities to help each child in your class KNOW and FEEL you love him or her. Show genuine interest in each child and his or her activities and accomplishments. Learn children's names and use them frequently in positive ways.

Social

Children are concerned with pleasing their teachers. Each child is struggling to become socially acceptable to the peer group. The Golden Rule is a tough concept at this age. Being first and winning are very important. Taking turns is hard. This skill improves by the end of the second grade. A child's social process moves gradually from *I* to *you* to *we*. **Teaching Tips:** Provide opportunities for children to practice taking turns. Help each child accept the opinions and wishes of others and consider the welfare of the group as well as his or her own. Call attention to times when the group cooperated successfully.

Intellectual

There is an intense eagerness to learn and children of this age ask lots of questions. They like to repeat stories and activities. The concept of time is limited. Thinking is here and now rather than past or future. Listening and speaking skills are developing rapidly; girls are ahead of boys. Each child thinks everyone shares his or her view. Children see parts rather than how the parts make up the whole and they think very literally. **Teaching Tips:** Consider the skill and ability levels of the children in planning activities. For example, some can handle reading and writing activities and others may do better with music or art. Use pictures to help them understand Bible times and people. Avoid symbolism!

Spiritual

Children can sense the greatness, wonder and love of God when helped with visual and specific examples. The non-physical nature of God is baffling, but God's presence in every area of life is generally accepted when parents and teachers communicate this belief by their attitudes and actions. Children can think of Jesus as a Friend, but need specific examples of how Jesus expresses love and care. This understanding leads many children to belief and acceptance of Jesus as personal Savior. Children can comprehend talking to God anywhere, anytime in their own words, and need regular opportunities to pray. They can also comprehend that the Old Testament tells what happened before Jesus was born and the New Testament tells of His birth, work on earth and return to heaven and the works that occurred afterwards on earth. **Teaching Tips:** The gospel becomes real as children feel love from adults. Teachers who demonstrate their faith in a consistent, loving way are models through which the loving nature of God is made known to children.

What to Expect from Kids in Grades 3 and 4

CHILDREN

Physical

Children at this level have good large and small muscle coordination. The girls are still ahead of the boys. Children can work diligently for longer periods but can become impatient with delays or their own imperfect abilities.
Teaching Tips: Give clear, specific instructions and allow children as much independence as possible in preparing materials. Assign children the responsibility for cleanup.

Emotional

This is the age of teasing, nicknames, criticism and increased verbal skills to vent anger. At eight years children have developed a sense of fair play and a value system of right and wrong. At nine years children are searching for identity beyond membership in the family unit. **Teaching Tips:** Here is a marvelous opportunity for the teacher to present a Christian model at the time children are eagerly searching for models! Provide experiences that encourage children's creativity and self-concept. Let all the children know both verbally and by your actions that "love is spoken here" and that you will not let others hurt them nor let them hurt others. Make your class a safe place to be.

Social

Children's desire for status within the peer group becomes more intense. Most children remain shy with strangers and exhibit strong preferences for being with a few close friends. Some children still lack essential social skills needed to make and retain friendships.
Teaching Tips: This age is a good time to use activities in which pairs or small groups of children can work together. Create opportunities for each child to assume increased responsibilities.

Intellectual

Children are beginning to realize there may be valid opinions besides their own. They are becoming able to evaluate alternatives, and are less likely than before to fasten onto one viewpoint as the only one possible. Children are also beginning to think in terms of "the whole." Children think more conceptually and have a high level of creativity. However, by this stage, many children have become self-conscious about their creative efforts as their understanding has grown to exceed their abilities in some areas. **Teaching Tips:** Encourage children to look up information and discover their own answers to problems. Provide art, music and drama activities to help children learn Bible information and concepts. Encourage children to use their Bibles by finding and reading portions of Scripture. Bible learning games are good for this age, and these are good years for Bible memory work. Help children understand the meaning of the verses they memorize.

Spiritual

Children are open to sensing the need for God's continuous help and guidance. The child can recognize the need for a personal Savior. There may be a desire to become a member of God's family. Children who indicate an awareness of sin and concern about accepting Jesus as Savior need careful guidance without pressure. **Teaching Tips:** Give children opportunities to communicate with God through prayer. Help them understand the forgiving nature of God. Talk personally with a child whom you sense the Holy Spirit is leading to trust the Lord Jesus. Ask simple questions to determine the child's level of understanding.

What to Expect from Kids in Grades 5 and 6

Physical

Children have mastered most basic physical skills, are active and curious and seek a variety of new experiences. Rapid growth can cause some 11-year-olds to tire easily. **Teaching Tips:** 10-year-old boys will still participate in activities with girls, but by 11 years old they tend to work and play better with their own sex. This is a good age for exploration and research activities. Use active, creative ways to memorize Bible verses.

Emotional

Children are usually cooperative, easygoing, content, friendly and agreeable. Most adults enjoy working with this age group. Even though both girls and boys begin to think about their future as adults, their interests tend to differ significantly. Be aware of behavioral changes that result from the 11-year-old's emotional growth. Children are experiencing unsteady emotions and often shift from one mood to another. **Teaching Tips:** Changes of feelings require patient understanding from adults. Give many opportunities to make choices with only a few necessary limits. Take time to listen as children share their experiences and problems with you.

Social

Friendships and activities with their peers flourish. Children draw together and away from adults in the desire for independence. The child wants to be a part of a same-sex group and usually does not want to stand alone in competition. **Teaching Tips:** Children no longer think aloud so keeping communication open is of prime importance. Listen, ask questions and avoid being judgmental.

Intellectual

Children of this age are verbal! Making ethical decisions becomes a challenging task. They are able to express ideas and feelings in a creative way. By 11 years children have begun to reason abstractly. They begin to think of themselves as adults, and at the same time question adult concepts. Hero worship is strong. **Teaching Tips:** Include lots of opportunities for talking, questioning and discussing in a safe, accepting environment. These are good years for poetry, songs, drama, stories, drawing and painting. Give guidance in a way that does not damage children's efforts in becoming thinking, self-directed people.

Spiritual

Children can have deep feelings of love for God; can share the good news of Jesus with a friend and are capable of involvement in evangelism and service projects. The child may seek guidance from God to make everyday and long-range decisions. **Teaching Tips:** Provide opportunities for children to make choices and decisions based on Bible concepts. Plan prayer, Bible reading and worship experiences. Involve children in work and service projects.

Write On!

Creative writing activities can provide valuable learning experiences for children when the experiences are planned according to the abilities of the child and when they hold no threat of failure. Committing thoughts to paper—as a poem, a story, a diary, a stanza to a hymn, etc.—aids a child in recalling and then developing the key thoughts expressed.

For example:

✦ A beginning reader may dictate words or sentences for the teacher to write, enabling the child to have a visible reminder of ideas expressed in class.

✦ A child who writes a letter to a friend explaining the main point of the lesson is developing skill in sharing the faith with others.

✦ A child who rewrites a Bible verse in his or her own words is grappling with meaning, not just rote memory.

✦ A child who contributes a word or phrase to a group composition is encouraged to feel a part of the class and enjoys the success of having his or her ideas accepted.

Benefits of Creative Writing Activities

Lesson-related creative writing activities can help children:

✦ list/describe specific concrete examples of an abstract concept such as loving, forgiving, worshiping, serving;

✦ express their feelings about God, or about their experiences and needs;

✦ synthesize their thinking as they put ideas into words;

✦ record ways they put Bible truths into practice in daily life;

✦ show love to others (for example, writing letters to missionaries or people who are homebound; writing thank-you notes to parents or the church staff; making "I will help you" coupons in which they offer to run errands, etc.);

✦ improve their recall of Bible events by organizing and writing information about the Bible story.

Tips for Leading Writing Activities

✦ Write on chalkboard or scratch paper any words that children need to know how to spell.

✦ Let a non-writer record his or her ideas on tape. Later, write or type these ideas and add them to the project being worked on.

✦ Let children work together, making sure one person in the group is skilled enough to write the ideas of the group.

✦ Ask a group to dictate a story or letter for you to write.

✦ A child's creative writing efforts are usually more productive when the teacher has done some "pump priming" to stimulate thinking.

✦ Show and discuss pictures or objects to get ideas flowing.

✦ Provide "story starters" (partially described situations which children build on or complete).

✦ Suggest a problem for children to solve.

✦ Before children begin writing, encourage them to talk about possible ideas they might use.

109

Discipline– Do It with Love!

What are the questions most frequently asked by teachers about children?

"How do I get children to behave properly?"

"What do I do when they get out of control?"

"What about the disruptive child?"

Fortunately, there are some guidelines to help answer questions about discipline. However, the answers really depend on teachers recognizing the relationship between the two dimensions of the word *discipline*—guidance and punishment.

Unfortunately, many people use the words *discipline* and *punishment* to mean the same thing. In so doing they miss the primary meaning of the word. Punishment is retaliation for wrong doing. Discipline is the process of providing guidance. Discipline helps a child acquire self-control—an inner commitment to do what is right.

Preventing Behavior Problems

"An ounce of prevention is worth a pound of cure." How much better for children when things go well and episodes of misbehavior and punishment are avoided! Consider the following ideas to make your classroom a "good place to be."

✦ **Develop an atmosphere of love and acceptance.** Each child who enters your classroom needs to feel loved and wanted. Children long to feel that someone cares about them, that they are people of value and worth. Sitting down and listening attentively to what a child has to tell, or kindly but firmly redirecting a child's out-of-bounds activity, are but two of many ways to demonstrate your love and care in ways a child can understand.

✦ **Provide meaningful activities.** Children need to be actively involved in interesting things to do—not just required to listen or observe for the entire session. Children often misbehave simply because they are bored when there is nothing new or challenging to engage their minds.

✦ **Set realistic standards that can be enforced.** Be realistic and consistent in what you expect children to do or how you expect them to act. For example, recognize that a child's ability to sit still is limited. So provide physical activities and changes of pace in the schedule that allow children to release pent-up energies. Children also need the security of knowing you are consistent in the way you maintain a standard of behavior.

In planning Bible learning experiences, establish realistic goals. For example, if a child is unable to learn an entire verse, focus on a portion of the material and help the child achieve success in that activity.

✦ **Recognize accomplishments and good behavior.** "I really appreciated how you..." or "You're really good at..." are two ways to affirm your students. Encourage all children; not only those who are often behavior problems, but also those who have already achieved a high degree of self-control. When children know they will receive attention for positive behavior, their display of disruptive behavior often diminishes.

(Continued.)

Discipline— Do It with Love!

(Continued.)

Correcting Behavior Problems

There are occasions when corrective measures are necessary. In dealing with a behavior challenge, we can do one of two things— ignore it or respond to it. There are times when ignoring the problem will be the best solution. Many children would prefer our negative attention to no attention. Often we are guilty of making an issue of matters that would be better left alone.

When we cannot ignore misbehavior, here are five helpful steps to follow in correcting the situation.

1. Deal with the problem individually. Avoid embarrassing the child in front of friends. When possible, talk with him or her alone.

2. Have the child tell what he or she did. Don't ask why the child behaved in that way. A "why" question merely invites the child to attempt to justify the offense. Perhaps you will want to tell what you saw and then ask, "Is that what happened?" Deal only with the current situation. Do not bring up past offenses.

3. Be sure the child understands why the behavior is not acceptable in the classroom. Either ask the child to tell why the action is a problem, or offer a clear explanation of the reason you intervened. Phrase your explanation so the child can recognize the problem as his or her own, and that it results in a loss to the individual and to the group.

4. Redirect the child in positive behavior. Focus on good behavior. For example, ask, "Corrie, can you think of a better thing you could have done?" or "What can you do about it now?" Then help the child implement positive changes. As the child makes these changes, give honest and sincere encouragement to reward acceptable behavior.

5. Let the child experience the consequences of behavior. Attempt to tie a child's actions to natural consequences. When materials are misused in the classroom, we can remove the materials from the child, or we can remove the child from the materials. Let the child choose whether to correct behavior voluntarily or to lose a privilege or some other response appropriate to the offense.

Your positive, loving approach to the needs of your students is one of the most important factors in making your classroom a good place to be. Guiding a child to learn self-control and to demonstrate obedience to parents and teachers is a first step to the ultimate goal of helping the child learn obedience to the Lord. Pray for understanding, wisdom and patience. Be a loving, caring person both inside and outside the classroom, no matter what the behavior challenge may be. "If you love someone you will...always expect the best of him" (1 Corinthians 13:7, *TLB*).

Bible Learning with a Dramatic Flair

Drama activities such as role-plays, skits, puppets, pantomime, etc. are valuable learning opportunities because of the process the child experiences, not because of the quality of the final performance. Bible stories come alive when children act them out, and Bible truth is seen to be relevant when applied to contemporary situations.

Benefits of Drama Activities

✦ A child portraying a Bible character will clearly recall what that person said and did.

✦ A child speaking through a simple puppet may express thoughts and feelings that would not likely be spoken otherwise.

✦ Planning and then acting out a situation will push children to think about the application of Bible truth to a real-life circumstance.

✦ Dramatic activities provide a unique opportunity to briefly step into another person's shoes, and experience for the moment some of his or her attitudes and feelings.

✦ Acting out specific examples of loving, sharing, kindness, friendliness, caring and helping gives concrete meaning to these otherwise abstract words.

Tips for Leading Drama Activities

✦ A good way to introduce drama in your class is to begin by reading the Bible story narration while class members pantomime the appropriate action. Later, students may read dialogue parts in the story.

✦ If possible, provide a dress-up box of fabric and simple props to help stimulate children's thinking.

✦ Plan for an area in your room that can be cleared of furnishings and used as a stage for the dramatization.

✦ If children feel unsure of themselves, they will sometimes try to cover up their insecurity by acting silly To prevent this:

✦ Start with very simple stories/situations with a minimum of dialogue.

✦ Talk over the story/situation in enough detail so children feel sure of what to do.

✦ Demonstrate how a specific part or action might be acted out or pantomimed (or let a volunteer do this). Then let several children show how they would do it.

✦ If a child pauses during the drama, ask a question to help him or her remember the action of the story or think of what to do next.

✦ Don't force a child to act out a story or situation, but do involve him or her in other ways: planning, evaluating, prop-making. Encourage participation by suggesting that a shy child take a part with little or no speaking.

✦ When presenting role-plays of contemporary situations, provide several alternatives of ways a character might respond to the problem presented. Allow children to choose the option they feel best illustrates the concept being taught.

What Does Your Classroom Say to a Child?

CHILDREN

A classroom is that silent partner that has the potential to aid or hinder student learning, to enhance or distract from even the best curriculum and teaching methods. Children's classrooms need to reflect order, friendliness and space for a variety of learning experiences. Consciously or unconsciously, teachers and students are influenced by their classroom environment.

Your Equipment

Appropriately sized furnishings are important if the child is to be comfortable and able to learn efficiently. The height (floor to chair seat) for chairs should be 12-14 inches (30-35 cm) for first and second graders and 14-15 inches (35-37.5 cm) for third, fourth and fifth graders. For sixth graders chair height should be 16 inches (40 cm). Tables should be 10 inches (25 cm) above chair seat height.

Survey the furnishings in your classroom. If they are too small or too large, exchange furniture with another department so that all benefit. If this exchange is not feasible, ask a carpenter in your church to adjust chairs and tables to correct heights. Painting and repairing furnishings can be done with the combined efforts of parents and teachers.

Your Room

From the time a child enters your classroom, the surroundings affect that child's attitude and resulting learning. The effect may be positive or negative. Bend down so you can see the room from the eye level of the child. As you look around the room objectively, consider these questions:

1. How do you feel about entering the room? Do you want to come in?

2. Is the room neat and clean? Does the air smell fresh?

3. Is the room colorful and light?

4. Is there something in the room that is particularly attractive to you?

5. Do you feel encouraged to become involved in an activity, or is everything so sterile you are reluctant to touch anything?

6. Are there windows you can easily see through?

7. Can you find and return the materials you need?

8. Is there space enough to move around without bumping into furniture?

9. Are the bulletin boards and chalkboards at the eye level of the students? Does the material displayed on the boards encourage Bible learning?

As you answer these questions, list the things you want to change in your room. Determine which of the adjustments you can do with little or no help. Then accomplish these as money, time, materials and space become available. Work around those things you cannot change.

If other groups use the room during the week, provide a room set-up sketch for your custodian so the major furnishings can be properly arranged each week.

(Continued.)

What Does Your Classroom Say to a Child?

(Continued.)

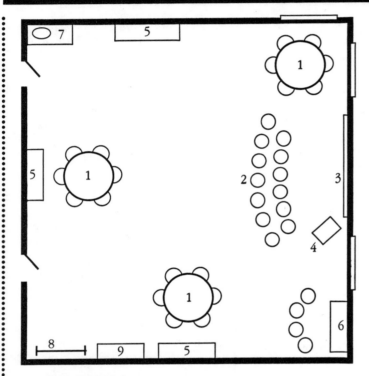

1. Table and chairs to seat 6-8 children for Bible learning activities.
2. Chairs (used at tables) grouped for Bible sharing time.
3. Bulletin board with picture rail.
4. Small table for leader's materials.
5. Low shelves for materials (glue, paper, crayons, etc.).
6. Bookshelf with several chairs.
7. Storage cabinet and sink counter.
8. Coatrack.
9. Shelves for take-home materials.

DIAGRAM 1
Open Room
Arrangement

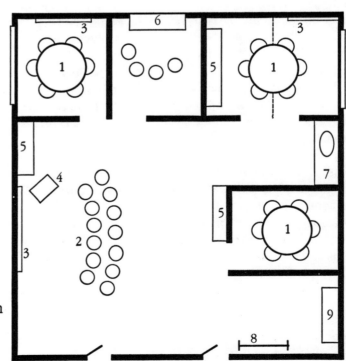

DIAGRAM 2
Assembly/Classroom
Arrangement

Everyone's a Winner in These Games

CHILDREN

Play and learn! Often children are not aware of the direct learning value of a game, but they participate enthusiastically because they enjoy the game. Bible games are helpful tools for involving children in an enjoyable way to discover, use and remember Bible truths and verses.

For example:

♦ matching Bible words with their definitions can give the teacher opportunity to ask children to tell of times they do or do not show the quality of the word they defined;

♦ playing "20 Questions" (students ask yes- or no- questions to discover the answer) about Bible characters can lead children to think of varied actions or qualities of each character;

♦ Bible verse puzzles give repeated opportunities to review the meaning and application of the verses.

Benefits of Bible Games

Through Bible games the child can:

♦ discover new information;

♦ review Bible truths;

♦ develop skill in using the Bible and research materials;

♦ reinforce skills through practice;

♦ apply Bible truths;

♦ memorize Bible verses;

♦ increase his or her skill in interacting in a group situation (taking turns, being fair and honest).

Tips for Leading Games

1. Explain rules clearly and simply. It's helpful to write the rules to the game. Make sure you explain rules step by step.

2. Offer a "practice round." When playing a game for the first time with your class, play it a few times "just for practice." Children will learn the rules best by actually playing the game.

3. Choose games appropriate to the skill level of your class. If you know that some children in your class are not able to read or write as well as others, avoid playing games which depend solely on that skill for success. When playing a game in which students must answer questions, suggest that the student whose turn it is may answer the question or ask a member of his or her team to answer the question.

4. Vary the process by which teams are formed. Allow students to group themselves into teams of three or four members each. Play the game one time. Then announce that the person on each team who is wearing the most (red) should rotate to another team. Then play the game again. As you repeat this rotation process, vary the method of rotation so that students play with several different children each time.

How Well Do You Know Your Children?

CHILDREN

Name of child

_____

1. **Briefly describe this child's family.**

Parent(s) Names:

_____

_____

_____

_____

Interesting Information:

_____

_____

_____

_____

Brothers/Sisters (place in order of birth):

_____

_____

_____

_____

Other information you know about the child's home situation that will help you teach and relate to the child.

(Continued.)

2. What school subject does this child like most? Least?

3. What is child's favorite activity?

4. Is child a Christian?

5. Name two of child's closest friends from church.

6. How does child feel about coming to your class or program?

7. What character quality concerns child's parents most at this time?

8. What lesson or activity has interested child most in recent weeks?

Guiding Children's Conversation

CHILDREN

Guided conversation is an important way to help children learn at church. Guided conversation is informal discussion during classroom activities that directs the child's thoughts, feelings and words toward the lesson focus. Think carefully about your conversation during classroom activities, because those moments are filled with the potential for meaningful learning. Be alert to ways of relating the child's experience to what God's Word says, thus helping that child understand Bible truth.

Conversation with individuals and small groups also helps a teacher build a good relationship with each child. Children need to feel that you love each of them and are interested in the things that interest them. As you guide the conversation, look for opportunities to express praise and encouragement. Each child needs to know that you recognize his or her honest efforts and the things he or she does well.

> *Use conversation to direct the child's thoughts, feelings and words toward the lesson focus.*

Your conversation with children helps you discover what information a child knows (or doesn't know) about a particular topic. Engage children in a dialogue rather than a monologue. As children work on an activity, look for ways to make comments or ask questions to help children understand new words, ideas, Bible customs and facts he or she will encounter throughout the session.

> *Conversation needs to be a dialogue rather than a monologue. Listen more than you talk.*

Finally, guided conversation should stimulate rather than interfere with the child's learning experiences. The learning process is enhanced when you help the child relate Bible truths to his or her own experiences.

Think of ways you might tailor or build upon any conversation ideas in your curriculum to more specifically meet the needs of your own class. You will then be able to take advantage of those teachable moments that occur spontaneously during a session—opportunities that are uniquely yours.

Here are some guidelines for using guided conversation effectively.

1. Be prepared. Read the information in your teacher's manual. Become familiar with the lesson focus. Review any conversation suggestions provided. Write several other questions you might ask. Keep these with you during the session.

2. Stay with your children as they work. The children need to know that you are there, ready to listen and ready to talk.

3. Know the characteristics of the children you teach. Be aware of individual differences in maturity. Be sensitive to each child's home situation and plan your conversation to include the variety of family situations represented in your class.

4. Recognize and accept the ways children respond to guided conversation. Some children are quite verbal. Others may respond with nods or other motions.

5. Spend more time listening than you do talking. Look directly at the child who is talking. Demonstrate your interest in what was said by responding to the specific ideas the child expressed.

The opportunities for guided conversation with children are endless. Prepare thoughtfully and prayerfully during the week. The Holy Spirit will use your words to reveal God's love and truth to your students.

The Teaching-Learning Process

CHILDREN

Ministry to children is enhanced when we understand and plan experiences to meet the following basic steps in a child's learning process.

1. Listening

An essential and basic learning task is listening or giving attention. The teacher seeking to initiate the learning process must first get the attention of children. Gaining interest often involves motivating the student through both the room environment and student activities which introduce the material to be studied. For example, a simple poster with several questions to be answered links to a game which will help students discover the definition of a key vocabulary word. The poster and game combine effectively to gain a child's attention and "want to" at the beginning of a learning experience. Most children listen better when they are alerted to something specific they should hear: "There are three things you need to do in playing this game. Listen carefully to make sure you don't miss one."

2. Exploring

The second step in the learning process, exploring, involves the careful investigation of a problem or subject. The student needs to become an explorer, involved in the search for something not yet known or experienced. He is not a passive listener or mere spectator but a central and active participant. Much of the exploration children need to do involves using the Bible or other study aids. Exploration may also involve posing questions, defining problems or suggesting possible approaches to dealing with life situations.

Steps to Learning

1. Listening: Secure the attention of the student.
2. Exploring: The student investigates a problem or subject.
3. Discovering: The student discovers for him- or herself what the Bible says and understands its implications for his or her own life.
4. Appropriating: The student identifies what God expects of him or her in daily situations.
5. Assuming Responsibility: The student changes his or her behavior or feelings in order to obey God's Word.

3. Discovering

As a result of the listening and exploring processes, the student discovers for him- or herself what the Bible says. Then, guided by the Holy Spirit, the student understands the Bible's implications for his or her own life.

Discovering God's eternal truths in His Word is an exciting process. Too often the teacher is the only one who makes these discoveries. Although the teacher may excitedly share them with the students, why shouldn't the joy of discovery also be the child's as he or she is guided by a skilled teacher? Time constraints may limit how many discoveries children can make during a session, but time should not be an excuse for simply trying to "cover the material" without involving children in the process. The goal is to have children learn and apply Bible truth, not "cover the material."

(Continued.)

The Teaching-Learning Process

(Continued.)

4. Appropriating

Once the child has discovered the meaning of the Scripture passage, he or she needs to think in a personal way about the truths involved. The student must relate the meanings and values discovered to his or her own experiences. Bible knowledge that is not being examined for its personal implications is not accomplishing its God-intended purpose.

Guide the child's task of appropriating, or making Bible truth his or her own. Bring up a real-life problem to solve on the basis of a biblical truth. For example, "Josh loved baseball and was playing the last inning when he realized that it was past dinner time. He knew his parents would be waiting for him, but he did not want to leave the game. What should he do? What does the Bible tell us about this kind of problem?"

Personally appropriating the Bible truth of a particular lesson enables the student to recognize its meaning for his or her own feelings and behavior. As a result of this step in the learning process, the student knows what God expects of him or her in situations related to this truth.

5. Assuming Responsibility

This is the crown of the learning process, the place where the previous tasks—listening, exploring, discovering and appropriating—culminate. Here God's truth actually changes and molds a child's thinking, attitude and behavior. For it is at this point that our efforts to communicate God's truth should result in changed lives. Our children must be led to actually do certain things on the basis of what they have been experiencing (in the previous steps of the learning process). The true test of learning comes when a child voluntarily uses what he or she has learned in new situations. This may involve practicing a quality of behavior in the middle of class activities (being kind, friendly, sharing, helping, forgiving, etc.). It may also involve planning service projects or other opportunities to put Bible learning into action. At other times, it may be best to have students plan specific actions to take during the coming week.

The process of human understanding and learning is summed up in these steps to learning. Listening, exploring, discovering, appropriating and assuming responsibility are not simply activities in which students are to be engaged but are inseparably bound together with Christian teaching/learning goals and objectives. Through the Holy Spirit's guidance of a thoughtful teacher, the spiritual dimension of a child's personality can continue its growth and development.

Motivate Your Students to Learn

CHILDREN

There is a direct relationship between a child's motivation to learn and the effectiveness of the learning process. How can we motivate children to want to learn?

Consider these suggestions for motivating children. Although not every idea will be effective with every child, never give up! As long as communication between teacher and student exists, there is an opportunity for increasing a child's desire to participate and to learn.

Learning Checklist
✦ **How does each child feel about being in your class?**
✦ **Do both you and the children look forward to studying God's Word together?**
✦ **Does each child feel your acceptance and support?**
✦ **Is there an atmosphere of warmth and happiness?**
✦ **Is there an opportunity for each child to succeed?**
✦ **Are choices provided?**
✦ **How do you insure a relaxed pace, free from time pressure?**
✦ **How are you helping children build relationships with one another?**
✦ **Are your expectations of children realistic and consistent?**

1. Know your students. This concept can never be overemphasized. Become well acquainted with each child in your class. Know individual interests, abilities and skills. Your insights will enable you to increase motivation for participation and learning as you help the child to recognize abilities, utilize skills and respond to areas of personal interest. Very often a seemingly unmotivated student will gladly participate in activities that capitalize on his or her interests and abilities.

2. Plan for children to have a choice of activities. When a child is allowed to choose between equally acceptable options, the act of choosing is in itself a way of increasing interest. Allowing choices of ways to complete an activity (e.g. deciding on use of chalk, paint or crayons for a mural) also increases interest and motivation.

3. Provide opportunities for children to interact and cooperate with each other. Most children respond favorably to working together in small groups, in pairs or in the total group. As children know each other better, motivation increases.

4. Listen attentively. An adult who listens to what a child has to say provides immediate incentive for that child to cooperate and participate in learning experiences.

5. Be flexible in your teaching procedure. Too much predictability leads to boredom for both children and teachers. Although a program needs stability, a good program is balanced by change and flexibility.

6. Provide opportunities for children to help other people. For example, a service project catches the imagination and enthusiasm of children as a first-hand way to put God's Word into action.

Strike a Chord with Music

CHILDREN

Benefits of Music Activities

A Bible Learning Activity involving music is an enjoyable way for children to be actively involved in learning and remembering scriptural truths. Music carefully selected for a specific purpose can help a child:

♦ learn Bible truths or doctrine;

♦ memorize Scripture verses;

♦ remember to display Christian conduct;

♦ feel an atmosphere of quietness and worship;

♦ move smoothly from one activity to another;

♦ enjoy relaxation and activity.

Music is often used with children as merely something to do until all the latecomers arrive, or as a change of pace from the real learning that is going on in the session. Such limited use of music misses the powerful impact music can have on children's understanding, remembering and applying Bible truth. While music is always an important ingredient in the worship segment of a session, it is also a valuable experience for a Bible Learning Activity group to participate in music.

For example:

♦ A Bible Learning Activity group may learn a new song in order to sing it for others in the department, sharing what they have learned about Bible truth through the words of the song.

♦ A group may compare the words of a song with the words of Bible verses to help them understand and recall the words of Scripture.

♦ A group may combine art and music by illustrating the words and meaning of a song.

♦ Children can identify times during the coming week when it would be helpful for them to remember a song they have learned to sing, or have illustrated, or have accompanied with instruments.

Tips for Leading Music Bible Learning Activities

♦ Ask the following six questions about any song you intend to use.

1. Is the meaning obvious to children?
2. Is it easily singable?
3. Does the song relate to the current unit of Bible lessons?
4. Are the words scripturally and doctrinally correct?
5. Does the song build positive attitudes?
6. Will children enjoy it?

♦ Invite a member of your church choir, or a parent who is musically skilled, to lead a music activity during one or more lessons.

♦ Use the music cassette provided with your curriculum to help you become familiar with a song.

♦ Ask if a child in your class has an electronic keyboard he or she could bring to class to use in accompanying a song.

You Can Lead Music!

CHILDREN

"I'm just not good with music." Have you ever heard (or said) those words? Using music in the classroom is a very real problem to many teachers. The problem afflicts teachers who do not have an accompanist, who lack confidence in their own singing voices and who find it hard to decipher an unfamiliar melody, especially if they do not read music. If any of these descriptions fit you, you will find some very practical help in the next few paragraphs.

Keep in mind that musical excellence is not essential in providing good musical experiences for children. They identify more readily with an "ordinary" voice than with operatic beauty.

Learning a New Song

Many teachers tend to use a few songs again and again. "Those are the ones children like," is the common explanation. Which, when interpreted, usually means, "Those are the ones the children—and the teachers—know best." These suggestions will be helpful to you as you learn new songs:

1. Listen to the song recorded on the music cassette provided with your curriculum. Then sing along as you play the song again. Sing the song several times to become familiar with the words and the melody.

2. If you do not have a cassette tape of the song you wish to use, find a friend who plays an instrument to play the melody for you or ask a friend who likes to sing to teach you the song. Use a cassette tape recorder to preserve your friend's music.

3. Practice the song until you can sing it easily and confidently. Learn the song well enough so that as you sing, you can maintain eye contact with the children rather than look constantly at the songbook.

Teaching a New Song

Now that you are familiar with a new song, use the following steps to teach it to the children.

1. Letter the words on a large chart or overhead transparency, possibly decorating it with appropriate pictures. Hang the chart or project the words where children can easily see.

2. Capture children's interest before you introduce the song. You may connect the song to a learning activity in which children have participated that morning. For example, you might say, "We've been talking about names the Bible uses for God's Son, Jesus. Listen to this song to find another name for Jesus."

3. Present the song. Play the cassette as you and other teachers join in and sing along as a group. If you use an accompanist instead of the tape, be sure the accompaniment is simple, emphasizing the melody line.

4. Discuss children's answers to your previous questions or listening assignment. Focus on the main points of the song which children do understand. Then discuss any parts of the song that might be unfamiliar or difficult to understand. Ask questions such as, "What did the writer of this song want us to think about while we sing? Does the music sound happy? Serious? How does the music make you feel about what the song is saying?"

5. Ask children to join in singing the song. Sing only one stanza and/or chorus the first time. Plan to repeat the song in each session of the unit.

(Continued.)

129

You Can Lead Music!

(Continued.)

Adding Variety to Your Music

You may use the following suggestions to add variety and to encourage even more participation.

1. Add motions to songs. Children enjoy thinking of movements to indicate the meaning of words and phrases. Some songs naturally suggest expressive gestures.

2. Create new words to songs by leaving blank spaces for children to fill in. Or create a phrase in a song by letting children sing their own answers to a question in the song.

3. Provide other instruments, such as chimes, melody bells or a keyboard for children to use.

4. Lead children in choral speaking. Children respond well to the rhythmic speaking of songs. Any song can be used in this way. You may divide the class into two or more groups and assign each group parts of the song to speak.

Combining Art and Music

Using music with a variety of art experiences provides an added dimension to music in your classroom. Here are some ideas to try.

1. Make a rebus chart of the words of a song. Letter the words on a chart, leaving blank spaces where children can glue appropriate magazine pictures to represent words.

2. Make an illustrated songbook or frieze. Many songs can be illustrated in the form of a book or frieze (a series of pictures on a strip of paper). The words of each song phrase are written beneath a picture which illustrates it. Children may draw pictures or cut them out of magazines.

3. Make a mural about a song. Choose a song written with beautiful imagery which could inspire a colorful mural (a large picture that expresses an idea). Songs describing God's creation often contain appropriate phrases for illustration. Colored chalk or tempera paints are often used for murals.

Music is one of the richest and most natural forms of expression for both young and old. Scripture is filled with references to God's people responding in melody and rhythm. Remember to practice your songs until they are natural expressions of your own thoughts and feelings. Then present them to children with affection and enthusiasm. And don't be afraid to make some mistakes—your children will be delighted to see that you are learning, too.

Meeting Children's Needs

CHILDREN

God has entrusted teachers of children in the church with opportunities to help them learn vital scriptural truths. An effective teacher is aware of children's needs and how children grow and develop. An effective teacher is also aware of how these processes influence children's attitudes and actions—particularly as related to ways children learn best.

Their Needs

Love and Acceptance

A child develops a sense of value and worth—healthy self-esteem—through experiencing love and acceptance from parents, teachers and peers. The secure feeling of being loved is the foundation on which a child can build love toward others.

> *The child who feels loved by adults finds it easy to feel loved by God.*

While we may not always approve of a child's behavior, we can always accept that child as a worthwhile person. Approval and acceptance are two different concepts. Acceptance means recognizing another person's worth and feelings without judging or condemning. Acceptance does not mean permitting that person to engage in disruptive or destructive behavior.

Every child needs to feel unconditionally accepted *as is*, regardless of behavior or appearance. The child who feels loved and accepted by adults finds it easy to feel accepted by God. Avoid giving a child an impression that God will not love a child who behaves badly. God's love is a free, unconditional gift, offered to all, "even while we were yet sinners."

Choices and Challenges

Children are designed to learn in a variety of ways. Some of this potential goes unused because many teachers make no provision for new experiences. All too often teachers become so comfortable with a method or a procedure that their students can predict what will happen next and how it will happen. No wonder children are bored!

Allowing a child the opportunity to make choices increases motivation, which results in better learning. As you plan learning experiences, be sure to include activities that require a variety of skills. Allow for individual differences in children as well as their varying abilities in learning.

Once you have offered a choice, accept the child's choice. To ensure that you can accept the child's decision, plan and phrase your choices so the alternatives are equally acceptable to you. For example, if children will be drawing a Bible story mural, provide two types of drawing materials, such as colored chalk or felt pens, from which children may choose.

Praise and Recognition

Focus on a child's positive behavior by looking for his or her strengths—the things the child does well. Praise must be genuine! And praise must be specific. ("You put all the crayons away. Thank you!") Avoid vague expressions ("That's nice.") that leave the child unsure of what was done well. Praise for an honest attempt must be part of your relationship with children. Often teachers express praise only when the final goal is achieved; be sure to recognize the efforts of a child who tried, but did not complete the task. Acknowledge every effort, even small ones.

Independence and Responsibility

Children need increased opportunities to gain personal independence in order to become mature adults. Organize the classroom so students can take the responsibility for care of materials.

The additional effort and patience it will take to allow students to become increasingly independent and responsible will prove valuable to teachers and students alike. Not only will the children be given more opportunity to practice good patterns, but teachers will also benefit in the growing process, since their students will look up to them as leaders, rather than "enforcers."

131

Dialogue and Discussion

CHILDREN

Talking is a part of most other types of activities, but it can also be the major ingredient in a variety of interesting and valuable activities (brainstorming, interviewing, case studies, Bible reading, etc.). Many children respond well to activities that encourage them to verbally express their thoughts and feelings. Since the focus of oral activities is on what the child says, the teacher must phrase appropriate questions and then listen with sensitivity and understanding.

For example:

◆ Children enjoy thinking of questions to use in an interview of a Bible character, a church leader, an adult with specialized knowledge, a missionary guest, etc.

◆ Involving children in retelling the Bible story increases retention and gives children the opportunity to put the main truth the story conveys in their own words.

◆ Discussing ways of putting a Bible truth into practice can involve every child in offering ideas on the practical implications of God's Word.

Benefits of Oral Communication Activities

Oral communication activities allow children to:

◆ share their needs, interests, concerns, understanding (and misunderstanding), and possible solutions to problems;

◆ be heard by someone who will listen attentively to what they are saying. (Children are often with people who hear their words, but do not listen with understanding to what they are saying.);

◆ increase their listening skills;

◆ improve their Bible memory skills.

Tips for Using Oral Communication Activities

◆ Establish a procedure whereby children take turns being the "recorder" of any group ideas or discussions.

◆ When a child or group of children begin to dominate an oral activity, set guidelines. Say, for example, "Luis, we like to hear your good ideas, but we need to hear from two other people before you talk again."

◆ Give gentle encouragement to a child who is hesitant to participate. Begin by asking him or her a non-threatening question requiring a minimum answer. Then affirm the child's response.

◆ Suggest that each child turn to the person next to him or her to talk over a question or an idea.

◆ Children enjoy recording their answers to a question on cassette tape.

Making a Difference in Kids' Lives

CHILDREN

Finding the Children

In the past three (or six) months, how many new children have visited your class as a result of:
◆ planned leader or teacher outreach efforts?
◆ invitation by child in group (or child's parents)?
◆ invitation by someone in church?
◆ child's or parents' own initiative?
◆ child's participation in another church program (VBS, club, choir, social, etc.)?
◆ other?

Based on these answers, rate your efforts at finding new children:

    1—Excellent   2—Satisfactory   3—Needs Improvement

List the names, addresses and phone numbers of at least three children who could be prospects for your class. These may be children who have visited your class recently, children in your own neighborhood, children of church families who do not currently attend your class.

  1. Name: _____ Phone: _____

      Address: _____

  2. Name: _____ Phone: _____

      Address: _____

  3. Name: _____ Phone: _____

      Address: _____

Contacting Children

In the past three (or six) months, how many children have you personally contacted by:

VISITORS	REGULARS	
_____	_____	talking individually before, during or after class?
_____	_____	calling the child on the phone?
_____	_____	visiting the child in the home?
_____	_____	sending a personal letter or card?
_____	_____	inviting the child to your own home?
_____	_____	planning a class party?

Based on these answers, rate your personal efforts at contacting children:

    1—Excellent   2—Satisfactory   3—Needs Improvement

OUTREACH

Making a Difference in Kids' Lives

(Continued.)

How many of the visitors are now attending regularly? _____

How important were your contacts in gaining this attendance? _____

How many of the children who are not now attending might still be gained by further contacts? _____

Plan your contacts for the next three months. Set a goal for the number of out-of-class contacts you want to make each month:

VISITORS   REGULARS

_____   _____   Visits

_____   _____   Phone Calls

_____   _____   Cards and/or Letters

_____   _____   Other

Contacting Families

In the past three (or six) months, how many parents have you personally contacted by:

VISITORS   REGULARS

_____   _____   talking individually before or after class?

_____   _____   approaching them at other times around church?

_____   _____   calling on the telephone?

_____   _____   visiting in the home?

_____   _____   sending a personal letter or card?

_____   _____   inviting them to observe the class?

_____   _____   participating with the family in a social activity?

_____   _____   other

Based on these answers, rate your personal efforts at contacting families as:

   1—Excellent   2—Satisfactory   3—Needs Improvement

List ideas for getting acquainted with parents of children identified as prospects for your class.

Asking Questions Kids Will Want to Answer

CHILDREN

Questions that stimulate children's thinking are an important part of effective learning. The simplest kind of question requires a student to recall information previously received.

? Knowledge questions ("Who was Moses' brother?") do not stimulate discussion because once the question has been answered, little more can be said. Asking too many knowledge questions can stifle interest and decrease participation of those children who lack Bible knowledge or confidence in their abilities.

? Comprehension questions are designed to help a child interpret the meaning of information. For example, questions such as, "How do you think Moses felt when God told him to lead the Hebrew people?" or "What do you think was the hardest part about leading the Hebrew people?" require students to think before they respond. Because comprehension questions do not require "right answers," they encourage discussion rather than limit it. In fact, each student may suggest a different answer to the question, thus increasing the opportunity for discussion. Misunderstandings often come to light as well, giving the teacher opportunity to correct mistaken ideas. Never pointedly "correct" a mistaken idea; simply supply correct information.

? Application questions stimulate students to use information in a personal situation. For example, "When have you felt like Moses must have felt when God told him to lead the Hebrew people?" A student's response allows a teacher to know if learning is taking place. The teacher is able to determine if Bible truth is touching a child's daily life.

The use of all three types of questions helps a teacher discover what information a child knows (and doesn't know) about a particular topic and its particular implications. Conversing with children in the classroom needs to be a dialogue rather than a monologue. Check yourself to see if you listen more than you speak.

Building Relationships in the Classroom

CHILDREN

Some teachers just conduct classes. They tell Bible stories and lead activities. They prepare materials, mark attendance and keep order. Other teachers do these same things, but with an important difference. They also change lives. The children who are in their classes are never the same afterwards. What makes the difference?

Some teachers appear to attract children like the proverbial Pied Piper. These teachers seem to be gifted with a natural talent which others merely envy, convinced they cannot attain similar results. Fortunately, there are a few basic skills that can be learned easily and used effectively to build positive relationships with children. Teachers who practice these skills find their teaching becomes more enjoyable, and children respond openly to teachers who care enough to work at improving relationships.

Questions that require one correct answer can be threatening to children.

Skills for building relationships with children include both nonverbal and verbal skills. Some examples of *nonverbal skills* are:

1. Expression—Greet a child with a big smile and a warm greeting—and don't let it be the last smile of the day!

2. Posture—Sit at the student's eye level. Avoid hovering over children or moving mysteriously behind them. Join in the lesson activities whenever you can. For example, complete a worksheet, write a prayer or solve the code along with children.

3. Touch—Touching says, "I like you, you are worthwhile." Look for appropriate ways to build contact with each child through touch.

4. Gestures—Nod your head in response as a child talks with you. Lean forward to show interest. Gesture with an open hand. Include each child in the group with a broad sweep of the arms, or indicate specific children with a wave or nod.

5. Use of materials—A teacher can build children's confidence by demonstrating how to use unfamiliar supplies or equipment. The simple act of providing materials for children to use indicates a concern which children appreciate.

Some examples of *verbal skills* are:

1. Accepting feelings—Accepting means listening deeply, sensing and "feeling" the child's real emotions, and responding with honest empathy, even if not always with agreement. Say, "Darren says he sometimes hits his brother when his brother teases him. Darren, I know you must feel angry when your brother teases you." Later, in your class discussion you can refer again to this situation asking, "What is something helpful to do when your brother or sister teases you? What advice does today's Bible Memory Verse give for a situation like that?"

2. Accept ideas—Accepting ideas helps children dare to think out loud. It provides freedom to ask questions or express ideas, enabling children to expand their concepts.

3. Praise and encouragement—All children (as well as adults) need to feel good about themselves and what they are accomplishing. The most precious gift we can give a child (short of leading him or her to Christ) is a positive and realistic sense of worth and value.

(Continued.)

Building Relationships in the Classroom

(Continued.)

4. Open questions—Most teachers ask questions. However, questions that require one correct answer can be threatening to children. Open questions remove pressure by asking for opinions, feelings or ideas, not just facts.

5. Enabling directions—Instead of always telling a child exactly what to do, pose a question that allows the child to decide on a course of action. Instead of saying, "Put the glue on the shelf," you can ask, "Where does the glue need to be put?" Enabling questions help a child develop responsibility for his or her own behavior, building feelings of success and value.

These verbal and nonverbal skills are helpful for every teacher. Their use will more effectively communicate Bible truths and content while building many shared experiences between teacher and students. Initially, some of these techniques may seem awkward. However, with practice they will become natural and effective ways of building positive relationships with children—relationships that will carry over beyond the classroom.

> *Instead of telling a child what to do, pose a question that allows the child to decide.*

Leading Your Children to Christ

CHILDREN

1. Pray. Ask God to prepare the children in your class to receive the good news about Jesus and prepare you to communicate effectively with them.

2. Prepare a foundation. Your children are evaluating you and the Lord you serve by everything you do and say. They are looking for people who show a living, growing relationship with God, for people whose lives show that knowing God makes a noticeable difference, for people who love them and listen to them the same way God loves them and listens to them.

Learn to listen with your full attention. Learn to share honestly both the joys and the struggles you encounter as a Christian. Be honest about your own questions and about your personal concern for students. Learn to accept your students as they are. Christ died for each one while he or she was yet a sinner. (See Romans 5:8.) You are also called to love each one as is.

3. Be aware of opportunities. A child may show an interest in salvation by a direct question. However, he or she may be waiting for you to suggest going on an individual outing—getting alone together where you can share what it means to be a Christian.

4. Create a relaxed atmosphere. Here are some tips to keep in mind when you talk with a child.

a. *Put the child at ease.* Be perceptive of his or her feelings. Be relaxed, natural and casual in your conversation and avoid criticism.

b. *As the child talks,* listen carefully to what is said. Children sometimes make superficial or shocking statements just to get your reaction. Don't begin lecturing or problem-solving. Instead, encourage the child to keep talking and express him- or herself.

c. *Be gently direct.* Do not overpower the child with demands from the gospel. But make no apologies either. God does not need to be defended and neither does the truth. If a child does not bring up the topic of salvation, a simple question such as, "If a friend wanted to know how to become a Christian, what would you say?" can unlock a life-changing conversation.

5. Clearly and simply explain how to be a Christian. Discuss these points slowly enough to allow time for thinking and comprehending.

a. God wants you to become His child (John 1:12). Do you know why God wants you in His family? (1 John 4:8).

b. You and all the people in the world have done wrong things (Romans 3:23). The Bible word for doing wrong is sin. What do you think should happen to us when we sin? (Romans 6:23)

c. God loves you so much He sent His Son to die on the cross for your sin. Because Jesus never sinned, He is the only one who can take the punishment for your sin (1 Corinthians 15:3; 1 John 4:14).

d. Are you sorry for your sin? Tell God that you are. Do you believe Jesus died to be your Savior? Tell God. If you do believe and you are sorry for your sin—God forgives all your sin (1 John 1:9).

e. The Bible says that when you believe in Jesus, God's Son, you receive God's gift of eternal life. This gift makes you a child of God. This means God is with you now and forever (John 3:16).

Encourage the student to tell his or her family about the decision. Give your pastor the names of those who make decisions to become members of God's family. Students who make decisions need followup to help them grow in Christ.

NOTE: The Bible uses many terms and images to express the concept of salvation. Children often do not understand or may create misconceptions about these terms, especially those that are highly symbolic. (Remember the trouble Nicodemus, a respected teacher, had in trying to understand the meaning of being "born again"?) Many people talk with children about "asking Jesus into your heart." The literal-minded child is likely to develop strange ideas from the imagery of the words. The idea of being a child of God (see John 1:12) is perhaps the simplest portrayal the New Testament provides.

An Effective Teaching Schedule

CHILDREN

A successful teacher is continually alert for ways to use teaching time effectively. Follow these ideas to make the best use of time within the class session.

Total Session Teaching: What Is It?

Each part of your class schedule should contribute to the child's learning experiences. Just as all the pieces of a puzzle interlock to produce one picture, so should every part of your session fit into a unified purpose. Total session teaching focuses the entire session on a specific Bible truth and its application in daily living. Material not related to the lesson is eliminated, thereby allowing maximum time for lesson-oriented learning. This approach results in increased learning opportunities for the students because all information and experiences relate to one specific Bible truth.

A Proven Schedule

STEP 1
BIBLE STUDY
(25-35 minutes)

The uninterrupted and unhurried flow of Bible study at the beginning of the lesson when children are at their peak of learning efficiency increases the amount and depth of Bible learning.

The old saying that "Sunday School begins when the first child arrives" continues to be valid, regardless of a child's age or the size of the Sunday School. Immediately upon arrival, the child becomes involved in one or more **Bible Readiness** choices. These simple activities start the child thinking about the biblical concepts that will be developed in the Bible lesson. Offering the child a choice gets the child involved in accepting personal responsibility to participate and learn. Bible Readiness activities can usually be completed in about five minutes.

Bible Story is the second part of the Bible study segment. During this time the teacher introduces the Bible story, weaving in opportunities for children to briefly share insights they gained from their Bible Readiness Choices. The Bible story time becomes much more than listening to a story; students become active participants by using their own Bibles to find the answers to

questions the teacher asks.

The third part of the Bible study segment is **Bible Application.** Here the teacher leads the children in discovering the relationship between Bible truths they have been studying and their day-to-day experiences. This experience is crucial to a child's learning! An exciting experience occurs when a child unlocks God's Word in terms of day-to-day reality!

STEP 2
BIBLE LEARNING ACTIVITY
(20-25 minutes)

When Bible study is complete, children immediately begin working on a **Bible Learning Activity**. A well-balanced session provides children with the opportunity to apply Bible truths to everyday living in a variety of ways. The activities also involve a child in using the Bible to review and reinforce information and concepts.

A Bible Learning Activity may involve art, music, writing, drama or other skills. But there is always opportunity for Bible research at the child's level of ability. These activities may be completed in one session or extended over an entire unit of lessons. Varied attendance patterns may make one-session activities more practical.

(Continued.)

STEP 3
BIBLE SHARING & WORSHIP
(up to 15 minutes)

Bible Sharing is the last segment in a total teaching session. The department leader or a teacher guides this time of songs, prayer, memory verse review and varied worship activities related to the lesson aims. Bible Sharing builds on what the children have been learning. It involves children in sharing what they learned about the Bible story, Bible verse and life application. This sharing adds another effective means of reinforcing Bible learning. Children may also show and describe their Bible Learning Activities.

Alternate Schedule: If two or more classes are studying the same course and are located in the same room, you may choose an alternate time schedule. The difference in this schedule is that **Bible Sharing** occurs in the middle of the hour rather than at the end. Each teacher offers a different Bible Learning Activity. At the end of Bible Sharing, children choose an activity in which they would like to participate. Not all children always get their first choice, as group sizes must be limited. However, the process of choosing greatly increases interest; as a result, learning improves.

What are the benefits of this alternate schedule? Moving from small class groups in the middle of the session to join another group helps children stay alert. It is also helpful for children to work closely with more than one teacher. Also, this plan allows children a choice of Bible Learning Activities.

Looking Out for Others

CHILDREN

Service projects allow a teacher to take a class beyond simply hearing about obeying God, talking about obeying God and even planning ways of obeying God. Acts of service done as part of a group are effective ways to help children actually begin obeying God by assisting others.

For example:

◆ A class may do an art, drama or music activity in order to benefit another class or group.

◆ Children may work together to care for church facilities (pick up litter, pull weeds, clean closets, sort pictures, etc.).

◆ Children may plan a class party to which they invite nonchurched friends.

◆ Children may adopt a "grandparent" in a rest home, or a missionary child their same age, or a child in a children's hospital.

◆ Children may collect canned foods, outgrown clothing, slightly used books and games to donate to a local missions organization.

Benefits of Service Project Activities

Service projects that grow out of Bible lessons can help children:

◆ encourage one another to do what God's Word teaches;

◆ experience the joy of giving to others;

◆ accept responsibility to complete a task;

◆ learn to work together;

◆ recognize that God's Word leads His people to action.

Tips for Involving Children in Service Projects

◆ Plan ahead to be sure your project is more than "busy work." Clearly explain to children how their work will benefit others. If possible, allow children time to brainstorm ideas to help others.

◆ If the service project will last more than a week or two, consider making a chart or poster on which to record your progress.

◆ Invite someone from the group that will benefit from the project to your class. Have children interview this person to learn about the needs they will be helping to meet.

◆ Involve parents or responsible teens to assist supervising children as they work on their project.

◆ Take pictures (photographs or videos) of children as they pull weeds, sort pictures, deliver canned goods, etc. Then display the photos in your classroom or show the video during a future class session.

Helping Children with Special Needs

CHILDREN

How do I handle the hyperactive child?

A clinically hyperactive child is different from a child who simply can't sit still for very long. The hyperactive child reacts to life the way you would respond to being closed in a room with the television, radio, stereo system, and two vacuum cleaners all turned up full blast. Sound like too much for you? A classroom often seems like "too much" for the hyperactive child.

Hyperactive children are unable to sort out and concentrate on one thing at a time. They are in constant motion mentally, and often physically as well. Since such a child is unable to sit and listen or even to work on one project for any length of time, he or she leaps from one distraction to another, and often distracts others at the same time.

In your ministry with children, hyperactive children need your special love and patience. Such children also need more adult guidance and attention, so plan for additional staff.

Be sure that hyperactive children are involved primarily in quiet activities which help them keep their energies channeled. Hyperactive children function best with a minimum of distraction and an activity which captures their attention.

As you show love to hyperactive children, be aware of the needs of the other children in your class at the same time. If your teaching is to have maximum effectiveness, you cannot allow one or a few children to distract others unnecessarily or reduce your classroom to chaos.

A hyperactive child may need individual attention from a teacher or a leader of your program. In some cases, it may be beneficial to enlist a caring adult to assist in the class and focus on meeting the needs of the hyperactive child. Consultation with parents as to the most effective ways to handle this hyperactivity can also be helpful.

How do I handle shy children?

A shy child may often feel insecure and afraid. It is important that such a child feel secure and loved. Encourage the children in your program to help others feel welcomed and important. This will happen as the leaders do it and teach by their good example. Do not refer to a child as "shy."

Do not push a shy child to talk in a large group. A rather quiet child will usually feel more free to talk in a small group in which every child is freely participating. Such a child may eventually feel free to speak up in a large group after he or she has had successful experiences in smaller groups.

Create situations where the shy child has the chance to successfully express him- or herself individually or in small groups. Encourage the child to tell about things with which he or she is familiar and secure. Direct questions to the shy child that he or she can successfully answer. The child may only be able to give short replies. But each successful expression will build acceptance and security.

Be sure that shy children receive your personal attention and encouragement, without being made to feel that they are "in the spotlight."

What about the aggressive child?

Again, the rule is to accept each child as he or she is. Every time there is positive behavior be sure that a child knows that you appreciate his or her efforts.

Your good example of showing love to others by encouraging and affirming them will also be helpful in teaching children how to relate to each other.

At the same time, you need to be concerned with the welfare of all children. If a child is being aggressive enough to upset or harm another child, firmly remove the aggressive child from the situation, and clearly explain the behavior necessary in order to return. Give the child the choice between obeying or "cooling off" for a longer period.

(Continued.)

147

Helping Children with Special Needs

(Continued.)

What about the child who says, "I can't"?

The "I can't" attitude is built on fear of failure. Children need the freedom to fail without loss of acceptance or status. Teachers can help children understand that "failure" is part of learning. Often it is necessary to discover what does not work, in order to find out how to accomplish the task.

"I can't" is often the student's way of saying, "Give me the attention I need to feel I can do this. Help me try a new experience."

Some phrases you can use to help children are:

"It's hard to try something when you're not sure you can do it."

"That does look hard. How much of it do you think you can do?"

"Make a start and see how it goes. Your work doesn't have to be perfect."

"This is a good place to practice something like this. No one will give you a grade or criticize what you do."

Avoid platitudes like "Do the best you can!" or "It's easy." Acknowledge the child's feelings and be sure the child knows you're on his or her side.

How should I treat the antagonistic or bored child?

Challenging children is a special task! Provide choices both in things to do and ways to do them. Increase interest through new experiences in the classroom. Discover the child's interests, then seek ways to incorporate activities that will appeal.

Accepting negative feelings may change the whole mood. Just a simple "Diego, I think you are bored," or "I think you're upset," will help a child know you are on his side.

Principles for Effective Storytelling

Storytelling scares more new teachers than perhaps any other facet of teaching. The prospect of having to capture the interest of squirming children and then sustain that interest for the duration of a story seems like a greater challenge than many people are ready to face.

Fortunately, effective storytelling is a skill that anyone can develop by practicing a few simple principles:

1. Have Confidence in Your Story

Why is this story worth hearing? Ask yourself this question to be sure you are clear on the value of the story to your class. People will listen to a story that offers them a benefit.

Ask yourself: What is the most interesting thing about this story? What are the features of this story that compel attention? What will my class be drawn to as they listen?

A few moments spent answering these questions can help you build confidence in the value and appeal of your story. When you are confident that the story has value and appeal, then you will be less concerned about your storytelling ability.

2. Prepare and Practice Your Story

Four essential steps should be taken in getting ready to tell any story:

✦ Identify where the story is going. If you are clear about the purpose of the story, you will be less likely to wander off the track. Your curriculum provides a lesson focus to help you identify the story's main point.

✦ Outline the story or read the outline provided in your curriculum, identifying the major events that occur.

✦ Review the story facts enough so that each point in the outline will remind you of the details involved in that event.

✦ Practice telling the story aloud using your outline to prompt you from one main point to the next. Tell your story to someone in your family, to a tape recorder or to yourself in the mirror.

3. Capture Interest at the Start

A good beginning is essential, because it is much easier to capture an audience than it is to recapture them after their attention has wandered. The surest way to kill interest is to ask, "Does anybody remember last week's story?" If this week's story connects in any way to last week's story, you can jog your children's memories as you proceed.

The best way to begin most stories with children is through some type of experience interesting to everyone in the group. This experience needs to connect to some aspect of the story. The younger your children, the more crucial it is to start a story with a reference to something in their own experience:

✦ Ask a question about something you know your children have seen or done. For example, to introduce the story of the wise men who followed the star, ask children to briefly tell of a time they looked up into a nighttime sky. Share your own experience to give children some insights into your life.

✦ Share a *brief* illustration to introduce your story. This could be an incident from your own experience, something recently reported in the news, or something you have read.

(Continued.)

Principles for Effective Storytelling

(Continued.)

◆ Involve your group in a readiness activity that prepares them for the story:

—A game that reviews information taught in previous weeks can help bring those who were present as well as absentees to a common level of information about events preceding today's story.

—Drawing a picture of a typical problem situation can get children thinking about the problem faced by a person in the story.

—Comparing distances on a Bible map with those on a local area map can help children understand the time and effort involved by the people in your story.

—Listening to a tape of a song can introduce children to concepts that are illustrated in the story.

—A sensory (touching, tasting, etc.) experience can arouse interest and appreciation for some facet of the story you are going to tell.

4. Identify Children's Level of Familiarity with the Story

Teachers face two opposing challenges in telling Bible stories to most groups of children. On one hand, there may be aspects of the story that are totally unfamiliar to children in your class. Customs, terminology, objects, relationships can all cause misunderstanding and confusion if not clearly explained.

On the other hand, some children have heard many of the Bible stories and may express boredom at the prospect of hearing "that old story again." An effective teacher keeps both these factors in mind in planning how to present a Bible story.

First, identify any aspects of your story you feel may be unfamiliar to at least some children in your group. It is usually easier to deal with these before actually telling the story narrative, rather than interrupting the flow of the story to stop and make an explanation. Second, recognize that at least some children have heard the story before; explain why you believe the story is worth studying again.

5. Focus Your Story

If you have ever tried to tell a joke, and then forgotten the punch line, you can appreciate the need for a clear point to every story. No matter how skillfully you tell a Bible story, it will have little impact unless the point of the story is clear to you and your class.

The stories in the Bible were intended to cause people to think and then to respond. No story was placed in Scripture just to provide entertainment. The stories should always lead us to consider our own lives in light of the good

or bad example we have studied, and then act on that consideration.

Unfortunately, some teachers get so involved in filling their stories with interesting tidbits and descriptions, that when they come to the conclusion, no one is too sure of what the story is all about. Most first and second graders, and many older children as well, cannot recognize the point of a story on their own.

The teacher must make the point of the story very clear to the children. To make sure the point does not get lost, tell the story so that the point is the focus of all that happens. If more than one main point is illustrated by a story, it is best to select one and emphasize it. One good idea, clearly communicated, is better than several good ideas that no one remembers.

As a general rule, the longer the story becomes, the harder it is to keep it focused. Therefore, keep your story brief. A good rule of thumb for a beginning teacher is to limit your story to one minute for each year of the children's age. If you have more than one age level in your class, target for the middle of the group, but be ready to shorten the story if the younger ones become restless.

(Continued.)

Principles for Effective Storytelling

(Continued.)

CHILDREN

6. Plan Your Story Sequence

Every story has five essential ingredients, each of which is needed in order for the story to make sense to children.

✦ **Setting**—Where did the story take place? In most stories this is the least important of the five factors. However, in Bible stories, stressing the setting helps children recognize that this event happened in the real world, not in never-never land or once upon a time.

✦ **Character**—Who is the main person in the story? If the main character has an unfamiliar name or occupation, take a moment to introduce him or her before starting the story. Present enough details about this person to help your audience care about what happens to him or her.

✦ **Beginning Event/Problem**—What happened to the main person? Something has to happen to set the main character in action and to get the listeners interested in what he or she is going to do. The problem should always be expressed in terms that make it relevant to the audience.

✦ **Action**—What does the main person do in response to the beginning event? If the audience is interested in what happens to the main character, they automatically want to know what he or she is going to do in the situation you have presented.

✦ **Result**—What happened as a result of the main character's action? If you are teaching younger elementary children, present the five parts of the story in their chronological sequence. If you teach older children, you may occasionally want to vary the sequence of the story parts. Also, your stories may be longer and have several cycles of events, actions and results.

7. Involve Your Group in Discovery

A good storyteller also includes opportunity for children to use their Bibles either before, during or after the story presentation. Help each child to:

✦ **Locate** the passage where the story is found. Even first graders can be helped to accomplish this task. Locating the passage in the Bible not only gives the child the sense that the story really is from the Bible and not from the teacher's imagination, but also begins to build confidence in learning to handle the Bible.

✦ **Read** something the Bible says. Rather than just asking a child to read a verse, ask the child to find some specific piece of information in the verse: a person's name, a word, a phrase, a statement, an answer to a question. Often the child who claims to already know the story will be surprised with something he or she reads in the Bible.

✦ **Understand** what he or she has read. Not until third or fourth grade do many children begin to read for "sense." Patiently guide children in this task by asking questions such as, "Can you think of another way to say that?" or "How would you explain that verse to a friend?"

(Continued.)

Principles for Effective Storytelling

(Continued.)

Make Your Story Come Alive!

Once you have planned your story, there are some skills you can practice to make your presentation most effective.

Try Something New with Your *Voice:*

✦ Try talking a little slower—or faster—to make parts of the story more dramatic.

✦ When the suspense builds, talk softer. A whisper is the most dramatic sound the human voice can make.

✦ On rare occasions, talk louder—but be considerate of other classes when you do.

✦ Above all, avoid talking down to the children. Talk to them as you would to your best friend. Be careful to use words your listeners understand.

Try Something New with Your *Face:*

✦ Make a conscious effort to smile as you talk, especially if you have a tendency to be very intense.

✦ Occasionally, try matching your expression to the emotion of a character in the story.

✦ Work at maintaining eye contact with your children throughout the story. Know your story well enough that you can glance at your Bible and your notes and then look up.

Try Something New with *Gestures:*

✦ Avoid nervous habits, such as scratching your head, rubbing your nose, fiddling with a tie or necklace, etc.

✦ Fold your hands in your lap or on your Bible until you need them to emphasize something.

✦ When you really want attention, gesture with your hands to invite the class to lean in closer to hear what you are saying.

✦ Occasionally touch a child's shoulder or hand to convey your interest and concern.

✦ Move closer to a child whose attention is wandering.

Try Something New with *Visuals:*

✦ Hold teaching pictures in front of you so that you can show them when you want to and then put them down when you want attention returned to you.

✦ Try mounting flannelgraph figures on craft sticks and using them as puppets.

✦ Invite children who already know the story to place figures as you talk.

✦ Ask children to tell what they think happened just before or just after the scene in a teaching picture.

Try Something New with Your *Presentation:*

✦ Show a short segment from a Bible story video. Preview the video before class.

✦ Use puppets to tell or act out the story. Involve children in using the puppets.

✦ Invite one or more children to tell the story, if they are familiar with it. Supplement their story with additional details.

✦ Lead the class in acting out the story.

✦ Invite a guest to portray the main character. Have children primed to ask the guest questions about the story.

Ideas for Summer Sunday School

CHILDREN

Does summer seem to be a time when you lose contact with many of the children in your class? Here's a helpful way to bridge the gaps created by vacation schedules.

Vacation Kit

Make a "vacation kit" of take-home papers, books, games and other items to give to each of your children when he or she travels on vacation. Such a kit helps you maintain contact with each child while he or she is on vacation and encourages each one to keep learning along with the rest of your class.

At the beginning of school vacation, find out which of your children will be going on vacation and when they will be leaving. Obtain a cardboard gift box or large manila envelope for each of these children.

Just before each child leaves for vacation, fill the box or envelope with items such as worksheets and/or take-home papers for the days the child will be absent. Other items you might include are ideas for games to play in the car or on an airplane, a box of crayons or felt pens and some paper. Your local newspaper may even provide a special children's section with coloring pages and other activities. Clip out the section to include in the kit.

Enclose a letter similar to the following in each vacation kit:

Dear (child's name),

In a few days you will be leaving for vacation. We'll miss you! But we know you'll have a good time.

Here are a few things to do while you are traveling—a book to look at, games to play, your Sunday School worksheets and take-home papers.

Have a happy vacation. And hurry home!

Your Sunday
School Teacher

Give a vacation kit to each child on the Sunday before he or she leaves on vacation. Explain the contents and purpose of the kit to the child's parents and encourage the child to use the materials inside. You might want to call the kit a "surprise box" and give instructions not to open the box until the child is a certain number of miles or minutes away from home.

Spice Up a Hot Sunday Morning

✦ Meet with your class in a shady spot outdoors.

✦ For a change of pace, stack up the chairs and have everyone sit on the floor.

✦ Bring a pitcher of ice-cold lemonade to serve before, during or after Sunday School.

✦ When children come back from vacation, take a few minutes during Bible Readiness or Bible Sharing to conduct interviews about where they went and what they did.

Teachers Take Vacations, too

✦ During the months of April and May, complete a "Vacation Calendar" that tells who will be gone on which dates.

✦ Update your substitute list.

✦ Recruit college students to teach during the summer. Ask mature high school students to observe in your class for one or two weeks. Then ask them to assist for a unit of lessons.

✦ Invite grandparents or others with no school-aged children or who cannot teach on a regular basis to substitute for a unit of lessons or the entire quarter.

✦ Combine classes on holiday weekends.

I Don't Wanna Go to Sunday School

PARENT/TEACHER

"Everybody ought to go to Sunday School, Sunday School, Sunday School. The mothers and the fathers and the boys and the girls, everybody ought to go to Sunday School."

When you read the words of this old-time chorus, what images come to your mind? A happy mother and father with 1.2 children cheerfully walking up the steps to church? A mother single-handedly struggling to get her children to the church on time? A continuing argument with a rebellious child who declares each week, "Sunday School is bor-r-r-ring"?

No matter what your situation, there is bound to be a time when you, as a parent or teacher, come face-to-face with a child's reluctance to attend Sunday School. For parents, it may start in the early years as you pry the clinging arms of a toddler from around your neck or listen to wails of despair as you hurriedly make your exit from the church nursery. Later on, as your child grows, you wonder how to respond when your son or daughter unexpectedly asks, "Can't we just stay home this week?" Sunday School teachers, too, feel moments of despair and frustration when they sense some children's unwilling attendance in their classes.

So, who's going to Sunday School? Everybody! And here are some guidelines for how you can make it happen in your family or class.

Don't Panic!

When you first hear the screams, complaints or questions, keep in mind that often the best approach is a light touch. A teacher or parent who threatens a reluctant Sunday School attender with God's disapproval or anger runs the risk of making a mountain out of the proverbial molehill. A matter-of-fact response will usually solve the problem. For example, a parent might answer, "In our family we always plan to go to Sunday School. You know, one thing I really like about Sunday School is getting to see some of my friends. Who is one of your friends at Sunday School?" Turning a negative complaint into a positive statement is a way to increase your child's enthusiasm for Sunday School. At some point, with an older child, a firm approach might be needed. "I know you would rather not attend Sunday School right now. But I think going to Sunday School is a really good way to keep learning about God and how He wants us to live. So we'll keep going to Sunday School."

Take Action

There are several ways in which parents and teachers can work together as partners to build a child's enthusiasm for Sunday School. Parents can often take the first step, especially if a child does not attend the same school as others in his or her class or has just recently begun attending Sunday School. Plan some get-acquainted times to help your child feel more comfortable in class. Invite another child and his or her family over for an informal dinner or a picnic in the park. It might even be helpful to ask your child's teacher over for dessert. Let your child know you are interested in what happens in his or her class. Ask to see your child's completed Sunday School worksheets. Take time to talk about them; memorize the Bible verses together. Before Sunday School, pray together asking God to help each one in your family enjoy a time of learning and worship at church.

Parents may find that sometimes a child may not enjoy Sunday School due to factors which cannot be changed. Your child may be the only girl in a class of boys or there may be a lack of variety in the class sessions.

In these circumstances, it helps to first acknowledge your child's unhappy feelings. Listen to his or her thoughts about Sunday School. Then you may be able to suggest several ideas to your child. It may be possible for you to help as a volunteer (lead a spe-

I Don't Wanna Go
to Sunday School

(Continued.)

cial activity, help with record keeping, act as greeter, etc.) in the class. Or you and your child may decide to invite the class to your home for a party. Encourage your child to invite a friend to attend class with him or her. Even while acknowledging to your child that the class may not be the most "fun" group in which he or she has been involved, it's important to focus on the positive rather than the negative factors.

A teacher who is aware of a child's reluctance to attend Sunday School might talk with the child or his or her parents to find out that child's particular interests or skills.

Planning a learning activity in which the child can use his or her skills will capitalize on the child's natural interest and abilities. Meeting with your class in a setting other than church (your house or a park) will build stronger friendships between the children and will help to overcome a child's unresponsive attitude.

Be an Example

It probably doesn't surprise you to learn that the greatest influence on a child's attitude toward Sunday School is the attitude and actions of the adults in the child's life.

Your decisions as a parent are signals to your child about the importance of Sunday School. A pattern of consistency in attendance and positive statements about the benefits of Sunday School will do more to affect your child's participation than anything else.

Teachers who demonstrate their enjoyment of Sunday School and exhibit a caring attitude toward each student will find a positive response in their classes. Both teachers and parents can let their enthusiasm for Sunday School overflow into the lives of children.

© 1992 by Gospel Light. Permission granted to reproduce.

The Church and the Blended Family

PARENT/TEACHER

Some people call them step families. Some people call them expanded families. Still others refer to them as remade or reconstituted families. Use whatever name you will, about 1,300 of them are formed every day. When the number of blended families and the number of single parent families are added together, the total equals the number of families in which an original husband and wife live together with their own biological children.

Blended families are not as noticeable as single parent families; they blend right in with everyone else. Most children of single parents will become part of a blended family, since the majority of single parents remarry. Often the blending of families is greeted with great rejoicing by the newlyweds, their relatives and friends. The establishment of new family relationships in a remarriage is generally viewed as a fresh beginning which can compensate for the losses experienced through divorce or death.

However, the blended family faces some unique challenges—challenges for which the church is uniquely able to provide practical help.

Special Problems of Blended Families

Blended families face all the challenges and problems experienced by any family; setting goals, household and income management, discipline of children, conflict resolution, etc. For a number of reasons, however, each problem has a greater potential for division in a blended family, especially in the first year.

✦ Stepparents and children tend to have very strong—and often unrealistic—expectations about how things will be. Some parents assume their new stepchildren will automatically love them dearly. Some children fear their new stepparent will be mean ("the Cinderella myth").

✦ The members of a blended family are attached to their previous family traditions and patterns of doing things. Just as it takes time for a new bride and groom to adjust to one another and it takes time for new parents to adjust to a newborn baby, it also takes time for members of a step family to become truly comfortable with one another.

✦ Discipline is more difficult because mutually accepted guidelines for sharing parenthood take time to develop.

✦ Children may be shuttled between families, creating scheduling pressures as well as conflicts between personalities and life-styles.

As a result of these and other uncertainties, it is not uncommon for children of blended families to exhibit unpredictable behaviors, sometimes seen as learning problems, disruptive actions, withdrawal or overly sensitive reactions. Many children may show no overt signs of trouble while holding in very deep fears, resentment or anxiety.

What Teachers Can Do to Help Children and Parents

Thoughtful teachers can help a child cope positively with the challenges of being a blended family.

1. Pray regularly for the child and the parents, asking God to help you become a supportive friend.

2. Be aware of the new situations and accompanying thoughts and feelings faced by a child in the months surrounding a remarriage.

3. Be aware of the ongoing schedule demands on a child who shuttles between two families on weekends, holidays and vacations. Make comments to build a bond of understanding: "It must be hard when..." or "I hope you have a really special time...."

4. In conversation, avoid assumptions regarding family life. Include references—without

The Church and the Blended Family

(Continued.)

sounding negative—to children who live in a blended family and who visit their other parent.

5. Plan specific ways to give the child some extra attention in every class session. Go out of your way to chat with the child about activities of the past week. Use the child's name. Affirm the child for effort expended and work accomplished.

6. Be patient about behavior challenges. Understand that the child may be trying to deal with significant disruptions. This does not mean allowing a child to run amuck. It does mean showing a great deal of love and acceptance.

7. If a child cannot attend regularly, mail the child's Sunday School worksheets and/or take-home papers, including a short personal note. Avoid making an issue of the child's absence; instead, focus on your interest in the child.

8. Work with others in your church to plan family events— game nights, overnight camp outs, movie nights, picnics, beach outings, etc. Enjoyable activities help blended families establish new traditions and create positive memories.

What Parents Can Do to Help Children and Teachers

Parents play a key role in helping the children in their blended family to develop strong bonds within the church family.

1. Be patient and flexible, both within your family and in guiding your family's interaction with others.

2. Openly explain your situation to your child's teachers. Show your desire to establish as much continuity as possible and invite ideas on ways to accomplish this.

3. To compensate for sporadic attendance, help your child build lasting friendships within the church family. Invite your child's teacher and/or children from your child's class to informal get-togethers. For example:

✦ A classmate will enjoy coming over to play after school.

✦ The teacher will be delighted to join your family for dessert at a favorite restaurant.

✦ The whole class will have a ball at a Saturday morning pancake breakfast and cartoon festival.

4. Keep your child informed of the routines. Preschoolers need constant reminders of what will happen next—just don't try to inform the young child too far in advance. The elementary-aged child, however, needs to know the long-range plan, e.g., "You'll be at Sunday School on the first and third Sundays of every month."

5. Talk positively with your child about why the church is important to you. And remember, your example will speak much louder than your words!

> *"Step" is derived from an Old English term meaning bereaved or despised. It's no wonder "stepmother" or "stepfather" conveys negative feelings.*

Childhood Is Not a Disease

PARENT/TEACHER

"Jesus said, 'Let the little children come to me, and do not hinder them, for the kingdom of heaven belongs to such as these.'" (Matthew 19:14, *NIV*)

The most striking thing about Jesus' encounter with these little ones is not that He interrupted an adult meeting to take time for some children. Nor is it surprising that He physically picked up the children and loved them. The remarkable part of this incident is Jesus' words. Most adults would have said something like "Let the little children come to me, and don't prevent them, for some day they will grow up and become important."

Jesus saw something in childhood besides the future. He recognized worth and value in the state of being a child, for He told the waiting adults in this crowd that children are important for what they are right now—"For of such is the kingdom of heaven."

We adults always seem to be looking to the future. This push for preparation robs childhood of much of its essence, as parents and teachers urge little ones hurriedly through the present in search of a more significant future.

The Future Is Now

"I know it's hard for a three-year-old to sit quietly and listen, but I have to start getting him ready for later when he will have to sit still."

"If he's going to be a success in life he'll have to go to college. And to make sure he can stay ahead in school, I'm going to teach him to read before he starts first grade if it kills us both!"

"If a child is going to grow up with an appreciation for the great hymns of the church, you just can't start too young to teach them."

These and many similar statements are used repeatedly by parents and teachers who are earnestly concerned about helping young children get ready for future roles and demands. However, these well-meaning adults sometimes actually do more harm than good, because in their long-range view of growth they have lost sight of the value in just being a child.

Children are more than people in transition, waiting for some future date of real meaning. The qualities that come from being young are not flaws or imperfections. Rather, childhood is a marked and definable stage of development.

"But an adult has so many capabilities and accomplishments far beyond those of a child. Surely the years of productive and responsible adulthood are more significant than those of infancy and early childhood."

What adult experiences could replace the laughter of children that gladdens the hearts of all who hear? How many hours of labor would it take to equal a little girl's smile? What a sterile world this would be were children not present to add their unique joys and sorrows!

The Value of a Child

Has any parent ever seen more deeply into him- or herself than when holding a newborn child and looking into the child's eyes? All the writings and research of humankind couldn't provide the insights that come with reliving the experiences of a child starting out on his or her own unique adventure. The child's fresh enthusiasm for everything seen, the child's honest questions and powerfully simple logic, all combine to peel the scales from our encrusted adult eyes.

What is the value of a child—as a child? Incalculable!

This is no plea for attempting to stop the progress of maturation. It is a call to recognize that just because a phase of life is brief, and is replaced by another more sophisticated, we should not rush past it. For if we bypass the unique

Childhood Is Not a Disease

(Continued.)

stages of childhood, we strip each succeeding developmental stage of some of its finest ingredients. The best preparation for any phase of life is the proper completion of the previous one. The second coat of paint must always wait for the first to dry. Harvest never begins when the first green shoots appear in the spring. Human life has an aching void when childhood is squeezed away.

Is this what Jesus had in mind when He took a small child in His arms and said, "I tell you the truth, unless you change and become like little children, you will never enter the kingdom of heaven" (Matthew 18:3, *NIV*). Is there a place in our homes and churches for children to be children? Do we wholeheartedly accept them as they are, not as we wish they were? Do the rooms and materials we provide sound out "Welcome!" to a young learner? Are the adults who surround young children deeply sympathetic and understanding of what these special years are all about?

Or do we merely see little ones in terms of their potential, enduring them until they get old enough to really matter? Is the church's objective in providing children's ministries a means of attracting their parents, or of getting ready for the church of tomorrow? Is our goal to train young children to act like miniature adults because their noisy spontaneity may somehow mar our sacred corridors?

W.C. Fields wrung many laughs from his famous line, "Anyone who hates dogs and kids can't be all bad." But have you ever met a person who wanted to live in a world where everyone shared Field's dislike of children?

It's far better to follow the Lord Jesus' pattern with children. His loving response to the children lets us see into His heart's feeling of the worth of a young life.

Childhood is not a disease to be cured or endured. It is a God-ordained part of human life with value and significance that continually enriches the experiences of those who may have forgotten what it is like to see the world from a fresh, unspoiled point of view.

> *Children are more than people in transition, waiting for some future date of real meaning.*

The Gimme Syndrome

PARENT/TEACHER

What Are the Symptoms?

What are the symptoms of the "gimme syndrome"?

An eight-year-old responds, "How much will you pay me?" when Mom requests her help.

A seven-year-old asks to invite more children to his birthday party so he can receive more presents.

A ten-year-old complains, "I wish we lived in a house as nice as the Garner's—AND they have three TVs!"

A five-year-old points out a multitude of toys and games she wants for Christmas.

Possessiveness and materialistic attitudes seem to be a hallmark of the twentieth-century child. The pursuit of money and possessions is glorified in many ways. Commercials, billboards, TV shows and movies all encourage children to believe that happiness can be bought.

What Is an Antidote?

What antidote can Christian parents and teachers administer to combat the disease of materialism in their children? Knowing that in God's eyes we are all the same, rich and poor, what can we prescribe for our families and Sunday School classes?

First and foremost, we can nurture an attitude of thankfulness in ourselves and in every child. James 1:17 reminds us that every good and perfect gift is from God. We need to do all we can in our homes and Sunday School classes to help children realize that our material possessions are not really ours, but God's. As you spend time with children, pause often for brief informal prayers of thanks to God. Begin a "thank you" list at home or in the classroom. Invite your children to add to the list often. Or, read the story of the ten lepers (Luke 17:11-19) and ask your children to think about ways they can be more like the one grateful leper. Then as a family or a class, take time once a month to write appreciation notes to people who have helped you.

Make sure your children overhear your expressions of thankfulness to God and to others. If you're thankful, say it!

Second, and perhaps more challenging, encourage your children to develop a non-materialistic attitude and life-style.

Take advantage of teachable moments. When your family receives an income tax refund, an unexpected gift or a Christmas bonus, use the occasion to talk with your family about good use of money—some to save, some to give and some to spend. And when the occasion is a lack of money rather than a surplus, you as a family can ask God's help in determining priorities for spending and express your reliance on His care.

The children of the Israelites regularly observed their parents bringing offerings of animals, food and precious fabrics and metals to the Lord. While our gifts are often not so tangible, children need to know what and why their parents give to the Lord. Your offering of a check once or twice a month, hours of volunteer labor or use of musical talents, for example, needs to be coupled with a brief explanation. You might say, "Helping to paint the worship building is a way I give to the Lord." Or, "God wants us to use our money in good ways. When I give this check to our church, I'm helping our church tell others about God. I'm glad to give this money because I'm so

The Gimme Syndrome

(Continued.)

PARENT/TEACHER

thankful for God's love to me."

Another way to help your children escape the "gimmes" is to plan ways for your children at home or at Sunday School to become aware of the extreme poverty in which millions in our world live. Show current newspaper and magazine pictures which depict the impoverished circumstances of others in third-world countries (or even your own country or community). Call your child's attention to TV news segments which highlight the needs of others. Avoid creating guilt (the "starving children in China" syndrome); simply offer information.

Then build on this awareness by providing a way for children in your home or class to act in a caring way for a needy person or family. As a family or class, plan and carry out a project to contribute to the well-being of others. Encourage your children to not only think about the needs of others in our world, but to follow your example in giving.

Consciously and unconsciously, children want to be like their parents. Your attitudes and actions now will make a difference in their attitudes toward money for the rest of their lives.

What About Christmas?

Many parents approach the holidays with a sense of dread at the overwhelming pressure to buy, buy, buy! Christmas celebrations do have a special attraction for children, and there's no point in simply wringing our hands over the way in which Christmas has become the most materialistic celebration of the year. Without diminishing the pleasure of Christmas and the joy of giving and receiving gifts, thoughtful steps can be taken at home and at church to increase the spiritual significance of Christmas for children.

The key is the attitude of the adults. If the spiritual quality of Christmas is not truly meaningful to parents and teachers, attempts to force sober observances and teachings on children will be self-defeating. Children take their cues primarily from those things that are of greatest interest to the adults in their lives.

Here are some specific ideas:

✦ At home you can set clear limits early in the season for gift-giving. Each child will benefit by realistic expectations.

✦ At church or home each person may secretly prepare a low- or no-cost gift for someone else.

✦ Encourage your family or class to participate in church, school or community giving projects.

What Is the Result?

The dictionary defines materialism as a preoccupation with or stress upon material rather than intellectual or spiritual things. Your efforts to cure the "gimme syndrome" will result in children whose value system is being changed—from a focus on selfishness to a focus on God and others.

Help Your Child Discover the Real Christmas

PARENT/TEACHER

Christmas! The word itself stirs feelings of extraordinary excitement. And rightly so. Everywhere there are reminders of the holiday season. But let's be sure our children know what the excitement is really about.

How can parents help a young child realize that Christmas is a celebration of gratitude to God for His wonderful gift of love? Here are suggestions for ways you can make the biblical and spiritual aspects of Christmas meaningful and attractive to your child.

Help your child know the simple facts of Jesus' birth as they are recorded in Scripture.

✦ Read the story of the first Christmas to your child from Bible storybooks or from an easy-to-understand version of the Bible.

✦ Visit your Christian bookstore and choose books and/or videos that will appeal to your child.

Help your child feel that Jesus is God's best gift of love.

✦ Remember that much of a child's response is a reflection of the attitudes he or she sees at home. Nurture feelings of joy, love and thankfulness in your child.

✦ Avoid (as much as possible) the hurry and busyness of Christmas that makes a young child feel alone or "left out."

✦ In the presence of your child, give thanks to God for Jesus.

✦ Include your child in family plans for expressing love to Jesus by caring and loving others. (Make cookies for elderly relatives, shut-ins, etc. Send cards to friends. Plan surprises for grandparents. Take canned foods or personal care items to a rescue mission, etc.)

Help your child express joy, excitement and feelings of love.

✦ Include your child in making Christmas decorations, foods, gifts and cards for family members and friends.

✦ Show gladness to your child as you sing the songs of Christmas. Find out and learn the songs your child is learning at church so you can sing them together at home.

✦ Be sensitive to moments when it is natural to talk about God and encourage your child to talk to God with thanks and praise.

Keep Santa in the proper perspective.

✦ Avoid referring to Santa as a real person. (Explain that Santa legends may be based on a real St. Nicholas who loved God and gave generously to the poor. A useful phrase is, "Talking about Santa is fun, and it's even better to talk about Jesus who loves us all year long.")

✦ Avoid the "What do you want Santa to bring you for Christmas?" and "Be good for Santa" emphases.

✦ When your child wants to talk about Santa Claus, listen attentively. Then say, "That's fun. Santa's a happy pretend fellow."

✦ Keep the meaning of Christmas clear by frequently commenting, "Christmas is a happy time because it is Jesus' birthday."

✦ Bake a birthday cake for Jesus. Children will understand that because Christmas is Jesus' birthday there should be a cake! Sing "Happy Birthday" to Jesus and plan together what your family can give Him for a gift of love.

Why Did Grandpa Die?

PARENT/TEACHER

When a child in your Sunday School experiences the death of a family member, a neighbor or even a pet, questions—expressed and unexpressed—are sure to arise.

"How does it feel to die?"

"What's a funeral like?"

"Why do people have to die?"

During the difficult time after a death has occurred in a child's family, parents and other relatives may be unable to adequately respond to a child's questions and comments. While there is no substitute for the love given to a child by his or her parents, a caring Sunday School teacher may minister to both the child and the family by being available to talk with the child or by giving a parent some appropriate comments to use in explaining death.

Questions and Answers

1. *What happens when you die?* "When a person or animal dies, it means the body has stopped working. Everyone will die sometime. Most people die when they get older. When you're old, you get sick easier and it's harder for your body to get well."

2. *Where do you go when you die?* "After a person dies, the body is usually buried in a cemetery. But the part of a person that thinks and feels keeps living. That part of a person is called the spirit. A person who is a member of God's family begins a new life with God in heaven."

3. *Why does God let people die?* "When God made people, He didn't plan for them to die. But when the first people on earth disobeyed God, sin—and death—became a part of our world. When someone dies, it reminds us how much we need God and His love."

4. *Does it hurt to die?* "Sometimes it hurts to die and sometimes dying is just like falling asleep. But no matter what happens to us, we know that God takes care of us and will always love us."

5. *What is heaven?* "Heaven is the place where God lives with all those who loved God and were members of His family when they lived on this earth. The Bible tells us that in heaven we will always be with Jesus and God. In heaven there is no sickness or death and no sadness."

"There is a place for you in heaven, too. God has prepared a wonderful home in heaven for all those who love Him and become members of His family."

6. *What will happen to me now that (Grandpa) has died?* In one form or another, this is the most urgent question the child needs to have answered. The child is deeply concerned about the void that has been left in the absence of a loved one. Reassure the child about the ways that void will be filled by people who love the child just as (Grandpa) did. "Everyone who loved (Grandpa) will miss him. But you can all keep loving each other just as you did when (Grandpa) was alive."

7. *Why do people have to die?* "Our bodies are not made to last forever. No one knows for sure when he or she will die. Most people live many, many years. Thinking about dying can be sad or scary. The important thing to remember is that God cares for you every day."

Conversation Tips

Don't be afraid to admit you don't know all the answers. You may want to preface a sentence of explanation by saying, for example, "I know it's hard to understand exactly what heaven is like. But the Bible has told us that in heaven we are with God."

Avoid telling a child that God "took" or "called" someone to heaven. Rather than comforting the bereaved child, such an explanation can make the child angry or fearful toward God for depriving the child of someone special.

Once the immediate crisis has passed, continue to acknowledge a child's questions or feelings of grief. Sometimes all that is needed is a simple statement of understanding. For example, "Jeremy, your grandpa died recently, didn't he? I'm sure you miss him. God knows when you feel sad and He understands how you feel."

Often a child may volunteer information about a death when a seemingly unrelated topic is being discussed. Take time to respond to the child's comment. Your interest and understanding will build a foundation for future conversations about concerns a child may face.

Divorce Happens to Children, Too

PARENT/TEACHER

by Kathi Mills

Within six months after my youngest son, Chris, was born, I heard about two couples in our church who were getting a divorce. I couldn't believe it! Christians didn't get divorced! What about the children? What about their Christian witness? What could these people possibly be thinking of?

And then, sometime later, it happened to me. Suddenly I was a single mother of three, the sole breadwinner for our household, the one whose responsibility it was to hold my children together physically, emotionally, and spiritually. Even as a Christian, it was almost more than I could handle.

After relocating, my children and I established ourselves in a large church where we knew very few people. Almost no one was aware of our situation, and I was reticent to tell them. However, a wise and perceptive Sunday School teacher recognized that Chris was having some problems in class, problems that she had seen before in children experiencing the stress of divorce.

Her phone call to me was a lifeline, not only for myself, but my children, as well. Because of her discernment and willingness to become involved, my children and I learned of a support group for families going through separation and divorce. The group met at the church once a week and provided the emotional stability and direction we needed to begin our journey back to wholeness. And it opened our eyes to the fact that we were not alone in our painful situation. There were many, many Christian families being torn apart by the ugliness of divorce.

What made this caring Sunday School teacher suspect our problem? She had noticed common behavior patterns in children going through divorce.

1. Outgoing, friendly children often become moody, withdrawn and sullen. They may erupt in tears or temper tantrums at the slightest provocation.

2. Children who were once quite secure in Sunday School may become frightened, crying and whimpering until the parent returns.

3. Children experiencing divorce may strike out at other children—hitting, biting, kicking, name calling.

4. These children may go off by themselves, refusing to enter into sharing times with others.

Although these symptoms are not always present in children experiencing divorce, and, if present, could be caused by other problems, they are behaviors worth noting.

If you think that one of the children in your class is experiencing divorce, what can you do?

1. If you know one or both parents well enough to feel comfortable approaching them with your concerns, do so carefully and with much prayer. Explain to the parent your concern about the child's behavior in class. Leave it to the parent to tell you only as much as he or she is willing to tell. Never pry.

2. If you discover that the child is indeed experiencing a divorce, be sensitive to the child's needs and behavior problems in class. Children of divorce need all the love and assurance they can get from the adults in their lives. A few hugs, some kind words, and a little extra attention can do wonders.

3. Find out about support groups available for families of divorce, either in your own or another church, or through the community. If the opportunity presents itself, be ready to offer that information.

You can't be expected to solve all the problems and heal all the hurts of the children in your classroom, but you can be sensitive to those problems and hurts. The sad fact is that divorce is not a problem confined to the secular world, but is in the Church, as well. You can be in prayer for these children and their families, asking God to show you what you can do for these children of divorce.

Kathi Mills is an author and editor who lives in Santa Paula, CA with her husband, Larry, and youngest son, Chris.

Making Easter Special

PARENT/TEACHER

Three-year-old Alan thought he had Easter analyzed. Confidently he explained: "It was when Jesus arose from the grave and the Easter bunny hopped out after Him!"

Easter is a joyful time, but it can also be a time of confusion for children as they get the secular and biblical aspects of the Easter celebration confused. Easter baskets, eggs and bunnies sometimes overshadow the true and beautiful Easter story from God's Word.

Jesus Is Alive!

"We are happy at Easter because Jesus is alive!" is what the children in your classroom need to hear from you often at Eastertime. Spring flowers, happy music, brightly colored eggs, gifts, even new clothes can all be made a meaningful part of Easter celebrations; help children understand that all of these things can be used to show and share joy because Jesus is living.

Long after Easter Day is past, the biblical truth that Jesus is alive is what children need to remember.

Keep It Simple

As adults, we need to keep in mind that words and phrases that are quite clear to us often have clouded meanings for young children. For example, "Jesus died and rose again" is not likely to have meaning or seem like a happy statement to little children.

Children have very vague and uneasy notions about what death involves. They usually see it as some kind of sad separation. Avoid dwelling on the gruesome aspects of the Crucifixion that may emotionally overwhelm young children.

Instead of dwelling on the details of Christ's death, help children grasp the great truth of the Easter story—a living Savior. You can help them understand by talking about the way Jesus' friends must have felt:

"Jesus' friends were very sad when Jesus died. Some of them even cried because they thought they would never see Jesus again. They were very happy when they found out that Jesus did not stay dead. They must have laughed and hugged each other. They told all of their friends, 'Jesus isn't dead. He is alive! Jesus is living.'"

As you talk about the first Easter, show appropriate Bible pictures from your Sunday School files or Bible storybooks. Talking with children about the pictures will give you opportunities to observe what is most important to them, clarify any misconceptions and build happy feelings about the Easter story.

As a child's ability to understand increases, so does his or her curiosity. As they hear about the first Easter, children may have several questions. The following suggestions will help you give meaningful answers they can accept and understand.

Why did they kill Jesus?
Jesus was hurt and killed by people who did not like Him. They did not know that God sent Jesus to love and help everyone. But God made Jesus alive again. Jesus is living! (See Matthew. 27:11—28:6.)

Where is Jesus?
He is living in heaven now with God, His Father. And everything is very beautiful in heaven. And everyone is very happy there. (See Ephesians 1:20 and Colossians 3:1.)

What is Jesus doing in heaven?
Jesus told us He is making a wonderful home in heaven. All who love Him (everyone in God's family) will be with Him in heaven someday. (See John 14:1-7.)

What is it like in heaven?
The Bible tells us that heaven is more beautiful than we can ever think. No one gets sick or hurt there. There is no sadness—only happiness! No tears—only happy faces and singing voices. (See Revelation 21.)

Will Jesus come again to earth?
Yes! But only God knows when it will be—some wonderful day! Everyone who loves Jesus (everyone in God's family) will be glad to see Him and to go with Him to the heavenly home He has made. (See 1 Thessalonians 4:14—5:10 and Acts 1:9-11.)

Making Friends— A Lifetime Skill

PARENT/TEACHER

*"Promises may get friends,
but it is performance
that keeps them."*
—Owen Feltham

*"A friend is someone you can
count on to count on you."*
—Anonymous

*"Unless you bear with the
faults of a friend
you betray your own."*
—Pubilius Syrus

*"Two are better than one....
If one falls down, his friend
can help him up. But pity the
man who falls and has no
one to help him up!"*
—Ecclesiastes 4:9,10 *(NIV)*

For thousands of years people have concerned themselves with the topic of friends. Who needs friends? Everyone! Who feels shy around people? Everyone! Surveys indicate that 90 percent of all adults experience shyness at least some of the time. Learning to make and keep friends is a skill we all need to develop. As parents and teachers, we are particularly concerned that the children in our homes and classes enjoy the support of friends. However, making and maintaining friendships is not something children succeed at automatically.

What Can Parents and Teachers Do?

At one time or another, most parents hear their child complain, "No one wants to play with me." Teachers may observe a child's unspoken feelings of loneliness or rejection by others in a classroom situation. While we cannot protect children from all unhappy experiences and feelings, there are some specific actions parents and teachers can take to help children develop friendships.

1. Talk—and listen—to the child. When a child complains at home or in class about a friend's actions, find out as much as you can about the situation and how the child feels. Begin by asking the child to tell you what happened. It's helpful to ask a specific question, such as "Where were you when...?" or "Who said that?" As a child tells the information, he or she may find it easy to also express feelings about the situation. (Parents, if you sense that your child is feeling "left out," but is reluctant to talk about his or her feelings, you may want to ask the child's teacher at school or church how the child gets along with others.)

2. Acknowledge the child's feelings. Offer a statement of sympathy to the child, agreeing that it's natural to feel sad about a friend's hurtful actions. "I know it's hard when a friend doesn't want to be with you." You may want to briefly tell an experience from your own childhood or describe how you feel now when a friend ignores you. Your understanding words will help the child know that you are on his or her side. However, be careful to keep your discussion balanced. Downplaying your child's feelings may make the child feel like his or her feelings are wrong; but overdoing your sympathy and involvement in the situation can make the child fearful that this problem may be overwhelming.

3. Take specific action.
   PARENTS:
   ✦ Ask your child to suggest someone he or she likes and who he or she would like to be friends with. Encourage your child to think of activities the other child enjoys. Then invite that child over to your home or to join a family outing. It may help if your child "practices" what he or she will say to invite a classmate.

   ✦ Involve your child in a new group activity, such as an after school program, community class, etc., in which your child will have the opportunity to meet some new potential friends.

(Continued.)

PARENT/TEACHER

Making Friends—
A Lifetime Skill

(Continued.)

✦ If your son or daughter complains that another child continually teases or makes fun of him or her, help your child realize that ignoring the teasing is usually the best way to discourage the teaser. Leave room for additional discussion by suggesting that if ignoring the offending behavior doesn't help, you will be glad to help your child plan another strategy.

✦ If you feel that your child is continually and actively disliked by his or her classmates, consider contacting a licensed child counselor recommended by your pastor or a school psychologist (every public school district is required by federal law to employ a psychologist). Your child may need a planned program of training in social skills. Your intervention at a young age may prevent a harmful pattern from developing.

TEACHERS:

✦ Plan one or more activities outside of the classroom. Sometimes children in a Sunday School class come from a variety of schools and/or communities. If the children in your class have limited opportunities to be together, an informal visit to the local mall or park can do much to build a bond of friendship in your class.

✦ When children are working on class activities, plan for them to work in pairs or trios. Form these groups at random. For example, children may choose colored slips of paper from a bag. Change the groups often. Or, if children are playing a Bible game, each time the game is played, change the teams. For example, ask the child who is wearing the most red on each team to trade places.

✦ Occasionally plan for children to participate in get-acquainted type activities, especially after children have moved to a new class. For example, you might make a word search using the names of the children in your class. Or, group children into trios; each group works together to make as many words as possible from the combined letters in their first names. Another idea: Letter several incomplete sentences on index cards. Children take turns choosing index cards and completing the sentences. Sentences might be, "My favorite subject in school is...." "I like to play...." "My favorite room in our house is...because...."

4. Pray. Take time to pray for and with your child or the children in your class. Ask for wisdom in talking with children about their friends. Emphasize that no problem is too small to pray about. Remind children of God's constant loving care for them.

What to Do About Halloween

Pumpkins, trick-or-treat, funny faces, scary masks—all symbols of the first holiday of the fall season—Halloween. Kids love it. Adults hate it, tolerate it, occasionally enjoy it, and for those of us who are Christians, are often confused as to our stand on it.

How Should Christians Handle It?

Should Christian parents and teachers encourage or discourage participation in the traditional celebrations of what is often considered a pagan holiday? If costumes and trick-or-treating are to be allowed, what are the limits?

There are as many answers to these questions as there are denominations in the Christian faith. One thing is certain, however. We cannot avoid the issue by ignoring Halloween. Children in public school, from preschool through high school, see and hear about the holiday for weeks ahead of time. Parties, costumes and trick-or-treating are discussed and planned in infinite detail.

Drugstores, grocery stores and department stores decorate their windows for the annual event, and advertise costumes and candy in newspapers and mailers.

It is inevitable that Halloween will be mentioned during conversations at home and in Sunday School. The important thing for the parent and teacher to remember is to answer any questions that may arise as openly and honestly as possible. A few facts about the history of Halloween might be helpful.

Where Did Halloween Originate?

In ancient Britain and Ireland, the Celtic festival of Sambain was observed on October 31. This was also the eve of the new year in both Celtic and Anglo-Saxon times. On this occasion, fire festivals were held, with huge bonfires set on hilltops to frighten away the evil spirits. The souls of the dead were supposed to revisit their homes on this day, so the festival acquired sinister significance. Ghosts, witches, hobgoblins, black cats, fairies, and demons of all kinds were thought to roam the countryside. It was the only day all

year that the help of the devil was invoked for divinations concerning marriage, luck, health, and death.

These pagan observances influenced the Christian festival of All Hallows' Eve, which was celebrated on the same date. Actually, the word "Halloween" comes from "All hallows' evening" ("hallow" meaning "saint"). Some churches recognize November 1 as All Saints' Day, a festival first celebrated in A.D. 610 when the Roman Pantheon was dedicated to the service of the Christian religion. Over the years, Halloween has become a secular observance, and many customs and practices have developed.

Halloween customs were introduced into the United States in the late nineteenth century, mainly by Irish immigrants. Mischief-making by boys and young men at that time was sometimes severe, even including major property damage. Eventually, though most of that died out, and trick-or-treating for candy took its place.

The jack-o-lantern, one of the most popular symbols of Halloween, also came to us from Ireland, although jack-o-lanterns were originally carved from turnips, rather than pumpkins. People in Ireland carved out turnips and put lights in them to scare away evil spirits. Soon after, children began making lanterns into faces to use on All Hallows' Eve.

(Continued.)

What to Do About Halloween

(Continued.)

What Are Some Alternatives?

Some parents, churches and schools offer parties on Halloween in order to provide children with a safe alternative to trick-or-treating. Bobbing for apples, carving pumpkins, encouraging cute, funny costumes (clowns, cowboys, firemen, ballerinas, etc.) as opposed to demons or witches, and stressing the idea of a "fall festival" atmosphere are all ways of dealing with Halloween, whether at a party, at home or at the church.

However you choose to handle the often-controversial issue of Halloween, it should be done in a positive and informative way, one that will not undermine the stand of your church or the personal convictions of parents or teachers. Take advantage of children's interest in this holiday to affirm your own deep faith in God's loving authority in all areas of life and His approval of all that is good and helpful.

Teaching Young Children About God

PARENT/TEACHER

Young children are curious. They are especially curious about God. They are curious about where He lives, what He wears, how He does things and when He will answer their latest prayer request. Because they are curious about God, they pick up many different things they hear and see, and early in life they form very definite ideas and feelings about Him.

Christian parents and teachers have the responsibility to provide young children with healthy guidance that will satisfy their curiosity. The best place to begin this process is for parents and teachers to consider the instructions of Moses.

The book of Deuteronomy shows Moses as an old man, standing before the nation of Israel. He is nearing the end of his career and his life. He knows that in a short time he will be gone and the people will finally enter the Promised Land.

What can Moses tell these people to ensure that their children do not forget all God has done? What system can Moses initiate that can effectively communicate God's laws and God's love?

Early in his message to Israel, Moses gave the clearest instructions in Scripture for introducing God into a child's life:

"And you shall love the Lord your God with all your heart and with all your soul and with all your might.

"And these words, which I am commanding you today, shall be on your heart; and you shall teach them diligently to your sons and shall talk of them when you sit in your house and when you walk by the way and when you lie down and when you rise up."

(Deuteronomy 6:5-7, *NASB*)

> **Teaching about God is the process of being an example of God in everyday life.**

1. Model Your Love for God

Moses started with the most important step. Teaching about God is first of all the process of being an example of God in everyday life. Moses told us to focus on loving God before trying to teach about God.

How can a parent or teacher communicate love for God in ways a young child can understand?

✦ **Talk about God around the child.** Do your children hear you talking about God with other adults? Do you give God enough of your attention that He is part of your patterns of thought and speech—even when you are not specifically trying to "teach" the child something?

✦ **Use your own Bible.** Before you start reading the Bible to your children, make sure they know you read it yourself. A book that you are interested in is a book they will want to learn about.

✦ **Use Christian music.** Records and tapes are great, but your own voice lifted in praise is far better. The melodies and rhymes of songs have an impact far beyond the words alone. And your enjoyment of the music makes its appeal even greater— whether you sing well or not!

✦ **Pray with children.** Pray naturally, simply and briefly about the things that interest children. Talking to God about scraped knees and other "minor" events conveys that God is interested.

(Continued.)

Teaching Young Children About God

(Continued.)

✦ **Demonstrate hospitality.** Mel Howell, one of the pastors at the Evangelical Free Church in Fullerton, California, says, "Many aspects of the Christian life are better caught than taught.... Christ calls us to demonstrate our love for Him by extending love and care to others." Many activities in Sunday School and at home provide a wealth of opportunity for children to observe and practice caring for others.

✦ **Build relationships.** As a parent or teacher demonstrates love and care for the child, the child develops the capacity to respond to the love and care of the heavenly Father. Gentle touch, warmth in the voice, eye-to-eye conversation and careful listening are all learned skills that adults need to develop in order to nourish the child's need for love.

2. Teach Diligently

Next Moses called for diligent teaching. This is not a hobby or an occasional pursuit. Moses knew that God would only become important in the life of a child if parents and teachers consistently presented Him to the child.

The first question many parents and teachers ask is about WHAT they are to teach. While there is much the young child cannot comprehend about God, there are many concepts that the child can grasp and that contribute to the child's healthy spiritual growth:

God created all things.

God loves everyone.

God sent Jesus.

Jesus died, but lives today.

God forgives me.

The list goes on, with the child's capacity for understanding growing as the child is surrounded by loving instruction from parents and teachers. Here are a few good rules of thumb in making WHAT you teach meaningful to a young child:

Keep it brief—attention spans are short.

Avoid symbolism—literal minds are at work.

Ask questions—let the child tell what he or she liked best about what you said.

Another practical issue of diligent teaching is WHEN to do it. Both teachers and parents should be alert to situations which can become natural teaching opportunities.

A third issue of diligent teaching is HOW to do it. Consider these tips:

✦ **Use variety.** Books, music and videos are great assets in staying out of a rut. If your resources are limited, check your church, school and local libraries—or arrange a swap with a church family.

✦ **Keep learning life-related.** Focus on concerns the child is facing today. The child needs a sense of God's interest in daily living long before the child needs a chronological understanding of the Bible or a theological definition.

✦ **Keep teaching times brief and simple.** A good rule of thumb is to limit teaching time to one minute for each year of the child's age. Trying to hold the attention of a three-year-old beyond three minutes is stretching, and you run the risk of having the child's interest drop off before you get to the key point you want to emphasize.

✦ **Be flexible.** Be willing to bend to meet the child's needs and interest. The goal is not to get the child to sit still and quit wiggling while the adult talks. The goal is for the adult and child to enjoy being together, learning to love God and each other.

✦ **Talk informally.** The word "teaching" usually brings to mind images of chalkboard, lectures, tests and homework. Perhaps a better word to use when considering God and young children would be "introducing." Think of how you would talk to a child about a dear friend you want the child to know and love. Long discourses are likely to make the child hope that "dear friend" never comes to visit. But brief conversations about that friend can arouse the child's interest.

(Continued.)

Teaching Young Children About God

(Continued.)

3. Ask Questions

Perhaps the best way to ensure that the child stays involved with and enjoys these conversations is to ask questions the child can answer.

✦ Which flower (tree, bird, animal, etc.) do you like best? If God has a favorite flower, what do you think it is?

✦ Why do you suppose God made snails (slugs, spiders, ants, etc.)?

✦ Which foods would you like to thank God for? Why do you think God made so many different things for us to eat?

✦ Which person in that story would you like to have for a friend? What makes someone a good friend? Why is Jesus such a good friend?

✦ What do you think might have happened in that story if the people had acted like God wants people to behave?

✦ What happened today that made you feel happy (sad, angry, etc.)? What could you tell God about what happened?

4. Answer Questions

It is not necessary that we be able to answer all the child's questions and fully explain everything about God. It is perfectly all right to point out that there are many things about God that no one knows. Since God is so much greater than any man or woman, there will always be things about Him no one can answer. Honestly admitting what we do not know is far healthier than trying to bluff our way through.

Once the child realizes that even grown-ups are in awe of God's greatness, he or she needs reassurance that, while we cannot know all about God, we can know some very important things about Him. As parents and teachers regularly affirm for the child what they do know of God, the child will grow to know Him also.

> *The goal is for the adult and child to learn to love God and each other.*

An Interview with Shirley Dobson

PARENT/TEACHER

Do you occasionally ask yourself, "What's the purpose behind all the glue, scissors and paper found in a typical Sunday School classroom?" Have you, as a parent or Sunday School teacher, ever wondered, "Is the effort of Sunday School worth it?"

Read on to find answers from Shirley Dobson to questions just like those.

How would you describe your childhood?

I didn't grow up in a home where there was a father and a mother who loved each other. My father was an alcoholic. He was one of the hundreds of thousands of alcoholics in this country and unless you've ever lived with it, you can't know the pain or the curse that it brings on a family.

Every Friday night my father would get his paycheck and head for the local bar and drink until every dime was gone. We did not have the family necessities we needed. There weren't enough clothes. There weren't enough shoes for school. And of course our house and our yard were literally falling apart. There was not a blade of grass in the front or backyard.

Some alcoholics take on a different behavior pattern when they are drunk. Some become very sentimental and cry easily. Some become loud and boisterous. They're the life of the party. But my dad would become violent. He had a terrible temper when he

was drunk. He would come in at 2 A.M. and threaten us until we were terrified. It was humiliating going to school the next day not knowing who knew that I had been up half the night with an incoherent father

How was it that you came to Sunday School the first time? Was your mother a Christian who attended church regularly?

My mother was not a believer, but she loved us and provided the only stability we had in our home. I'll always be grateful for her. She's a wonderful woman and has since become a deeply committed Christian. Even during my childhood, she had the wisdom to know that if she was going to raise these two kids without a husband she needed all the help she could get. And so she began to look around for a church. Not too far from our house was a little evangelical church in which she enrolled us.

I still remember my first Sunday School teacher's name—Mrs. Baldwin. She loved me! She was the first person in my life to tell me about Jesus. She told me that He loved me and that He knew me by name; that He gave up His life for me and that He'd seen all my tears. She told me that He was even preparing a mansion for me.

The first Scripture she had me memorize was: "In My Father's house are many mansions; if it were not so, I would have told you. I go to prepare a place for you. And if I go and prepare a place for you, I will come again and receive you to Myself; that where I am, there you may be also" (John 14:2,3, *NKJV*).

My heart was drawn to the Savior. When our pastor gave the altar call I went forward, knelt down and received Jesus into my life.

How did your new faith affect you?

For the first time in my life I had an anchor. My faith in Jesus gave me stability and purpose. I realized that I didn't have to be tossed back and forth with the circumstances of my life. I had a Friend to guide me and give direction through life. You cannot know what this message of hope meant to a child who was in such a hopeless situation. Here I was, caught in the chaos of a disintegrating family, and I heard a message that Jesus not only loved me, but that He has a plan for my life and someday I was going to have a mansion! It was a tremendous message of hope for me.

(Continued.)

PARENT/TEACHER

An Interview with Shirley Dobson

(Continued.)

What message do you have for Sunday School teachers today?

In every Sunday School class there are some Shirleys, just like myself. They may never know the gospel of Jesus Christ unless you personally give it to them. There's a place in a Sunday School class for crafts, for clay modeling, for coloring and other activities. But we must not forget the purpose for our teaching. It is to introduce children to Jesus Christ.

As Christians, our love for the Lord should be as contagious as the common cold. Has anyone caught "Jesus" from you lately? From me lately? That's our primary objective.

Let me also urge today's teachers never to underestimate the worth of a child, especially the one that comes from a broken home. I'm speaking of the kid whose clothes are shabby or whose hair is uncombed and whose parents don't come to Sunday School with him or her. Locked inside that child is a soul worth more than all the possessions of the world. Someday that boy or girl may remember you the way I recall my teacher, Mrs. Baldwin, and thank you for the contribution you made to his or her life.

Shirley Dobson is an author and homemaker. She has served as leader in Bible Study Fellowship, as director of women's ministries for her church, and has appeared on many radio and TV programs with her husband, Dr. James Dobson. She received an honorary degree, Doctor of Humane Letters, from Asbury College in May 1989. The Dobsons have two grown children and live in Colorado.

PARENT/TEACHER

You Are Vital to Your Child's Sunday School Experience

How to Help Your Child Get the Most Out of Sunday School

1. Encourage your child to develop friendships at Sunday School. One of the strongest benefits the church provides your family is an extended "family" of both adult and childhood friends who support positive Christian values. Consistent attendance makes it easy for meaningful friendships to grow.

2. Be consistent in bringing your child to Sunday School so that he or she will benefit from the biblical instruction. Children are surrounded by influences which are often in conflict with the truths of Scripture. Sunday School can be your child's most important hour out of every week!

3. Cultivate friendships with your child's teachers. It's easier for you to approach two or three teachers than for them to personally contact the parents of all the children in their classes. Your support helps teachers do a good job!

4. Watch for and talk with your child about the take-home materials provided each week. A few minutes of informal conversation at home can help to reinforce and apply the Bible truths your child has studied.

5. Learn the Bible memory verses with your child. Copy each week's verse onto a folded index card and set it on your breakfast table.

6. Ask a few questions about the Bible story to see what your child remembers and understands— and talk about how the story illustrates familiar experiences at home or in the neighborhood. A good question is, "What is one way you can do what that story teaches us?"

7. During the week look for ways to connect a recent Bible verse or story to specific situations. For example, while watching TV, ask how a character's action compares with those of a person in a Bible story.

How to Help Your Child Get the Most Out of Worship Services

1. Enter the worship building as a family, introducing your child to the adults you greet. This helps your child feel like part of the worshiping community.

2. Sit near the front so your child can see easily. Children tend to pay better attention and participate more the closer to the front they sit.

3. Before the service begins, take a few moments with your child to look over the order of worship in the bulletin. Comment on one or two things—unfamiliar or difficult terms, what the child should do at a certain time, why an item is included in worship, what meaning an item has for you.

4. Encourage your child to follow the order of the service. Ask your child to locate and read over the hymns or choruses ahead of time in order to identify unfamiliar words and phrases.

5. Share a hymnal, bulletin and Bible with your child. Holding a book together helps the child to feel a sense of participation.

6. If you are invited to shake hands with people nearby during the worship service, introduce your child to those you greet. Most adults tend to converse over the tops of children's heads, making children feel like outsiders.

7. Each week during the service ask your child to write answers to a question based on the Scripture passage, songs and/or the sermon. Questions might be, "What do you learn about God? What do you learn about how God wants us to act?"

8. After reading Scripture or singing a song, provide pencil and paper for your child to write a one-sentence summary of the Scripture or song. Some children may enjoy drawing pictures to illustrate a song or Scripture passage.

It's Never Too Soon to Pray with Your Child

The God of the Praying Parent

A child's first impression of what prayer is like may come from hearing Mom, Dad or a teacher pray. Hearing parents and other adults talk to God prompts the realization that God is someone who listens. A child learns an attitude toward God long before the reality of prayer has meaning. When a child consistently hears parental expressions of thanksgiving and praise for God's loving care, he or she quickly views God as someone loving and caring.

If talking to God in prayer is real to us, it will easily become real to our children. Your children will primarily learn about God and prayer by observing the process of prayer in you. Once a child begins to see God as a real person who is involved in Dad's and Mom's or their teacher's life—Someone who listens, cares and loves—the child will begin to talk to God naturally and spontaneously. God will become a constant Companion to your child, an ever-present Listener with whom your child can share all of the joys and sorrows of daily life.

You can also communicate the importance of prayer by telling your children about your own prayer experiences. Let them know when you are praying for them, and what you pray about. Also be sure to let them know when your prayers have been answered. Children will grow into a personal prayer experience if they see a consistent demonstration of its importance in the lives of their parents and teachers.

Talking to God

If your children are to have meaningful prayer experiences, they must know what prayer really is. Prayer is not the pursuit of a mystical experience, nor must prayers be phrased poetically to be pleasing to God. Prayer is simply talking to God. It's an attitude of the heart which is expressed in words, even in the simple words of a child.

In addition to using simple words in your prayers with your child, it is important to keep your prayer brief. A few short sentences give the child a model for prayer which is meaningful and which he or she can imitate. Long sentences and long prayers make prayer seem boring and not something for a child.

It's Never Too Soon (or Too Late) to Start

Parents and teachers often wonder when to start praying with children. We know that Jesus is vitally interested in children. When the disciples rebuked the people for bringing children to Him, Jesus replied, "Let the little children come to me, and do not hinder them, for the kingdom of heaven belongs to such as these" (Matthew 19:14, *NIV*). These children were brought to Jesus by their parents. Bringing children to God through prayer is something Jesus wants us to do, and the sooner we start, the better.

You can start now to introduce prayer by your example. Here's how one family began to pray together. These parents wanted to incorporate prayer into their family life and began at mealtime. At first they simply explained to their child that God had become an important member of their family, and they wanted to thank Him each time they sat down to a meal. That was the beginning. Eventually prayer was incorporated into other areas of their family life.

Tapping into God's Resources

One of the primary lessons about prayer which we must communicate to children is God's invitation to tap into His vast resources for the difficulties they face. When threatening issues come up, either from the neighborhood or the national news, discuss them with your children. Help them express their fears, anxieties and concerns, then help them tap into God's resources through prayer. Use Paul's instruction in Philippians 4:6 as a family watchword in anxious times: "Do not be anxious about anything, but in everything, by prayer and petition, with thanksgiving, present your requests to God" (*NIV*).

183

10-Second Teacher Training

Photocopy these mini-posters. Display them in classrooms, hallways and offices as reminders of key points about children's ministry. The mini-posters can also be made into transparencies for use in teacher training meetings.

The child who is the hardest to love needs it the most.

page 191

Love each child with your eyes, with your smile and with your words.

page 195

A picture is worth 1,000 words. An example is worth 1,000 pictures.

page 187

Teach as though the future depends on it— it does.

page 189

Talent, skill and personality are great. But God reserves His "Well-done!" for servants who are faithful.

page 193

Bring your Bible to class. Use your manual at home.

page 197

Ready or not your class begins when the first child arrives.

page 199

The child who most needs today's lesson may be the one who isn't here. Contact your absentees.

page 201

Focus on helping children do what is right, not just stop doing what is wrong.

page 203

Welcome to Our Resource Room

Please Use the Materials Available

1. If you borrow it, please return it.
2. If you spill it, please clean it.
3. If you empty it, please leave a note.
4. If you need help, please ask.

page 205

A picture is worth 1,000 words.

An example is worth 1,000 pictures.

Teach
as though
the future
depends
on it—
it does.

The child who is the hardest to love needs it the most.

Talent, skill and personality are great. But God reserves His "Well-done!" for servants who are faithful.

Love each child
with your eyes,
with your smile
and with
your words.

Bring your
Bible to class.

Use your manual
at home.

197

Ready or not your class begins when the first child arrives.

The child who most needs today's lesson may be the one who isn't here. Contact your absentees.

Focus on helping children do what is right, not just stop doing what is wrong.

Welcome to Our Resource Room

Please Use the Materials Available

1. If you borrow it, please return it.
2. If you spill it, please clean it.
3. If you empty it, please leave a note.
4. If you need help, please ask.

Cartoons

Add variety to your teacher newsletters by inserting one of the following cartoons. Cartoons can also be used in church bulletins, parent information newsletters and bulletin board displays.

Personally, I think Mr. Brown is carrying this visual thing a little too far.

page 209

Thy word have I hid in my heart...uh...that I might...get a star on my chart.

page 209

Is this really God's house?

Why, yes it is, Jimmy.

Then how come everytime I come, He's never home?

page 209

Let's put him in Mrs. Pennina's group. He hasn't bitten her yet.

page 209

What did you learn in Sunday School today?

Nothin! My teacher teached so long, it made me too tired to learn.

page 211

I stand alone on the Word of God, the ♫ B-I-B-L-E! ♫

page 211

Dear God, please help my Sunday School teacher to be able to get along without me this morning!

page 211

I asked Jesus to come into my heart so He got real tiny and slid down my tongue.

When I die, how will Jesus get out of my heart?

Jesus is in my tummy.

You tellin' me a black heart is bad?

Hic! Oops. I think... Jesus... Hic! needs more air!

page 211

Bible Learning Activities

Characteristics of Children

Bible Memory

Discipline

Learning

Music

Prayer

Salvation

Clip Art

JANUARY

 **FEBRUARY**

 **MARCH**

 **APRIL**

 **MAY**

 **JUNE**

 **JULY**

 **AUGUST**

 SEPTEMBER

 OCTOBER

 NOVEMBER

 DECEMBER

 SUMMER

 WINTER

 SPRING

 FALL

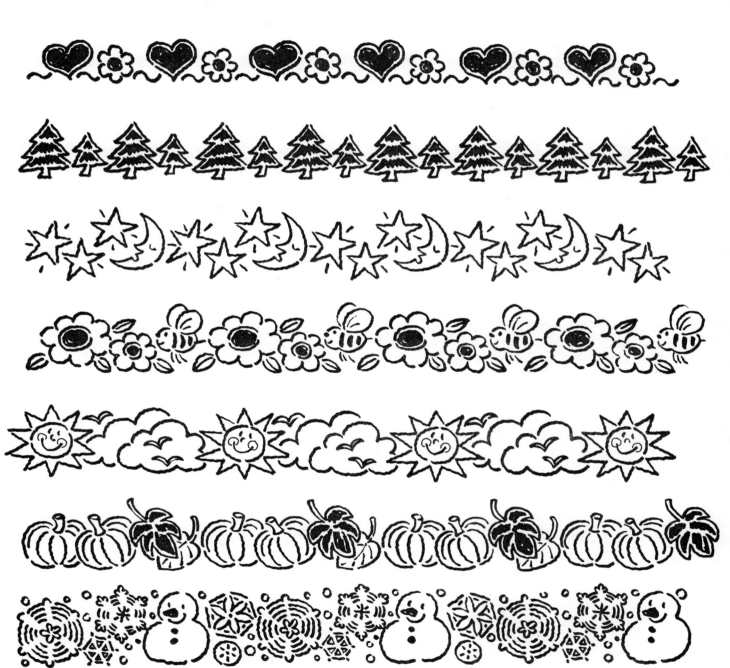

217

Notes   Teacher Training

CHILDREN'S MINISTRIES

STAFF NEWS   Staff News

SUNDAY SCHOOL NEWS

TEACHER NEWSLETTER

TEACHER UPDATE   TEACHER TIPS

TEACHER UPDATE   TEACHER TIPS

Additional Resources for Parents

BOOKS

***For Fathers Who Aren't in Heaven,* Ron Rand**

Most men don't lack motivation to become better husbands and fathers; here is help to put those desires to work.

***From One Single Mother to Another,* Sandra P. Aldrich**

These heartfelt and spiritually uplifting words will help guide single mothers past pitfalls such as loneliness, paying the bills, and raising children alone.

***Smart Kids, Stupid Choices,* Dr. Kevin Leman**

Kevin Leman blends a little humor and a lot of common sense to help parents guide their kids through the most tumultuous times of their lives.

***Talking with Your Kids About the Birds and the Bees,* Scott Talley**

This informative, inspirational and practical guide prepares parents and counselors to effectively shape children's sexual attitudes at any age.

***Teaching Your Child About God,* Wes Haystead**

Suggestions for parents and teachers to help children understand Christian truths and take first steps towards spiritual growth.

***The Power of a Parent's Words,* H. Norman Wright**

Teaches parents to use their words to help their children grow. Beginning with understanding a child's God-given personality, parents learn how to shape their communication and meet each child's unique needs with words of life and hope.

***The 3,000-Year-Old Guide to Parenting,* Wes Haystead**

If there's anything today's parents need it's wisdom. And who is wiser than Solomon? This up-to-date guide is packed with concrete ways to help parents strengthen their relationships with their children, insight on discipline and a host of other tips—all straight from the book of Proverbs.

AUDIOTAPES

***Discipline from Cradle to College,* Dr. James Dobson**

Positive and constructive discipline is a challenge for every parent. Dr. Dobson shares proven guidelines for learning to discipline with love. 6 Tapes

***Kids Need Self-Esteem Too,* Dr. James Dobson**

Parents can learn to strengthen their children's self-confidence and self-worth by example and good communication. 6 Tapes

***The Secret of Self-Esteem,* Dr. James Dobson**

Explores how we see ourselves and how important that is in our relations with others.

***Shaping the Will Without Breaking the Spirit,* Dr. James Dobson**

Learning to live a healthy and happy Christian life takes work. Dr. Dobson looks at how we need to understand our own needs as we accept changes in our lives.

(Additional Resources for Teachers on other side.)

Additional Resources for Teachers

AUDIOTAPES

15 Minute Teacher Training

Today's life in the fast lane makes it almost impossible to schedule teacher training. These concentrated training tapes sum up the essential of effective teaching in 15-minute bites, making them perfect for teachers on the move. Topics included are discipline, how to talk to children about salvation, understanding children and how to converse with children. Each set comes with two 30-minute audiotapes and is reproducible for you to provide a set to each of your teachers.

Series 1- Young Children, Ages 2-5
Series 2- Children, Grades 1-6

VIDEOTAPES

How to Teach Young Children About God

Here's a video training session for teachers *and* parents! *How to Teach Young Children About God* shows how to relate God's love in ways young children can understand. Teachers and parents will discover that they have an important role as partners in Christian education.

Hugs and Fishes

Put a curious, active boy alone in a room next to a goldfish bowl and what do you think will happen? *Hugs and Fishes* shows that even the wildest antics of children are really opportunities for sharing God's love. And amazing things do happen when ordinary people make a faith commitment to teach Sunday School. This video will inspire the members of your church to take a fresh look at Sunday School as a vital tool for developing the Christian leaders of the future.

CLIP ART BOOKS

The Big Picture Bible Time Line Book

These reproducible pages make a 60-foot time line showing the sequence of events in the Bible. Use for coloring activities or place around the room to help children track their progress through Scripture.

The Complete Bible Story Clip Art Book

Makes your lessons, flyers and handouts come alive. Includes pictures of Bible events, characters and places.

The Kids' Worker's Clip Art Book

Over 1,000 reproducible illustrations for teachers and others who love to work with kids.

The One Minute Poster Book

A dream come true for anyone who needs to publicize an event at church. It contains premade posters and flyers for every church event imaginable.

The Sunday School Clip Art Book

Produce great looking mailers, flyers, letters, invitations, brochures and announcements for your Sunday School. Follow the step-by-step instructions.

BOOKS

Everything You Want to Know About Teaching Young Children, Birth-6 Years, Wes Haystead

This handbook is designed to enable adults at church, home and school to better understand how young children learn and grow and how to meet their God-created needs.

Everything You Want to Know About Teaching Children, Grades 1-6, Barbara Bolton, Charles T. Smith and Wes Haystead

This handbook is designed to give the new as well as the experienced teacher fresh insights and practical plans for effectively teaching God's Word.